HIDDEN KILKENNY

JOHN KEANE

HIDDEN KILKENNY

KNAVES, KNIGHTS AND NORMAN ABBOTS

MERCIER PRESS

IRISH PUBLISHER – IRISH STORY

MERCIER PRESS

Cork

www.mercierpress.ie

ISBN: 978 1 78117 157 8

10 9 8 7 6 5 4 3 2 1

A CIP record for this title is available from the British Library

Printed and bound in the EU.

Contents

To my dearest Dor,
Lucy and Johnny

Acknowledgements

Thanks to Brian Keyes, editor of the *Kilkenny People* for his encouragement; to Rothe House, the Kilkenny Archaeological Society and the *Old Kilkenny Review*. The library in Rothe House is a wonderful resource and thank you to the staff: Mary Flood, Róisín McQuillan, Edward Law, Catriona Dowling, Daphne Coad, Victoria Barnes and Winifred Long.

Thanks to Susan Garret of Clomantagh Castle for her great assistance on that section and the one on Ballyspellan Spa, and for all her support. Thanks to Moira Cashin and her husband Joe for opening my eyes to a wonderful way of life in the thatched villages of South Kilkenny. And to Mooncoin (born Mick) Purcell in Idaho, USA – thanks for planting the seed and for the slogan: 'Guinness's for porter and the Purcell's for pigs'. To my mother for all her love and all my friends who didn't scold me about St Francis of Assisi (private joke too painful to share). Much of the history of Grannagh Castle is thanks to a wonderful article by Mrs T. G. Lanigan in the *Old Kilkenny Review* of 1960. Thanks go to Máire Ní Fhaircheallaigh of the Office of Public Works; to Damien Brett at the local studies section of Kilkenny City Library; and to Ben

Murtagh, archaeologist, renowned for his work in places like Kilkenny Castle and Grennan Castle.

I am indebted to Cóilín Ó Drisceoil and his late wife Emma Devine for their great work in investigating the Rathbeagh site, and Cóilín for his work on many of the pieces in this book. His help was invaluable. Thanks go to Margery Brady for her help and kindness in preparing the piece on Jenkinstown House and to Geoffrey Marescaux for giving such a wistful history of his family, the Swifts, in the *Old Kilkenny Review* of 1974. And thanks to the local man who knew all about the secrets of Swift's Heath. I'll leave a drink for him in the Fireside Inn, Castlecomer Road, Kilkenny.

I am indebted to Robert Duggan for his vast knowledge of Tybroughney; the local people owe him a huge debt of gratitude for piecing together so much about the castle and its hinterland. Mary O'Shea, another local historian, has done so much to enlighten us about our past in heritage-rich South Kilkenny. Patrick Comerford, writing in the *Old Kilkenny Review* of 1994, provided a wonderful insight into the life of the Comerfords after they left Ballybur Castle, and Canon Carrigan's history of the diocese was invaluable. Thanks to Billy Hoare for giving us so many of the songs associated with Brandon Hill. The book by Michael Holden, *Freney the Robber – The Noblest Highwayman in Ireland*, is a major addition to our knowledge of the master highwayman and it is referred to a number of times in this book.

There are few people as kind or as generous with their time and knowledge as Owen Doyle of Tinnahinch and his friend Colm Walsh. Thanks to Jackie Jordan of Kilkenny Castle for allowing me to sit and ponder the waterfall; to Maelle Champenois for a riveting and insightful tour; to John Walsh of Callan for filling in the blanks; to Noreen McDonald for reading the manuscript; and to Mr Kilkenny Castle, Frank Kavanagh, for his encyclopaedic knowledge of all things to do with the Butlers and the castle. Thanks also to the late Sean Power of Knockroe; Claire Goodwin of Kilkenny County Council for her time on Woodstock; Dr Breda Lynch for the tour of Jerpoint Abbey; John Kirwan for his advice; Gerry Moran for his encouragement; Eileen Little for her help and the painting of Jenkinstown Castle; Susan Mosse for letting me sneak into Kilfane, my Shangri-La; Gerry and Christine Byrne for allowing me to visit Kilcreene Lodge; Seán Maher for his help with Tory Hill; the beautiful Eoin Hennessy for his patience; Charlie Maher; Dylan Vaughan; Michael Keogh for being himself and showing me Dunmore Cave; the Great Scot, the miraculous Frank Gray of Ballybur Castle – hope the recovery continues; Jimi Conroy for illuminating all things to do with nature for me; Philip Cushen of Cushendale Woollen Mills for sharing the secrets of his art; the Byrnes of Mount Loftus; Liam Scott, Ian Doyle and Colm Murray of the Heritage Council located in the Bishop's Palace; the Cummins family, Rossenarra,

Kilmoganny, for tea, duck eggs and a mild scolding; to Brigitte Lennon (née Dorpmund) from outside Hanover, Germany, for maintaining Swift's Heath, Jenkinstown, with such perfection, enthusiasm and love; Cllr Tomás Breathnach for his passion for Grannagh Castle; Rhonda Evans, Ian Hamilton and Ronan Morrissey of Diageo and the St Francis Abbey Brewery; Denis Byrne, town sergeant of Kilkenny Borough Council, for allowing me in where I should not have been; Elizabeth Keyes of St Canice's Cathedral and staff, where 'there are no ghosts'; Shirley Lanigan for giving me hope; Gertie Keane for her passion and insight into Tudor Kilkenny; Damian Hogan of the *Kilkenny People* for his patience; the glamorous Norah Flynn and Marie Brennan at the front desk of the *Kilkenny People*; Billy Lahart for help with lots of things; and, finally, the Dowleys, for allowing me to roam around their home, Tybroughney Castle, with Robert Duggan.

Introduction

When I first mooted the idea of writing a series on the hidden heritage gems of Kilkenny for the *Kilkenny People*, my editor, Brian Keyes, was delighted. We drew up separate lists and then checked if either of us had come up with a few the other hadn't thought of on his own. It started from there and I plunged myself into the work.

Little did I think that the project would cause me such worry. By far the most beautiful private home in Ireland that I have seen is Castletown Cox, outside Piltown, County Kilkenny, and close to Carrick-on-Suir. I wrote the piece about it for the *Kilkenny People* and a few people said they had enjoyed it, people like Jim Brennan of the Club House Hotel, Patrick Street, Kilkenny. His wife's family, the Blacques, owned the estate at one stage. Then a bombshell. Someone had made an anonymous complaint about the piece to the police ombudsman of Northern Ireland, the police ombudsman of England and the gardaí. It claimed that I was subversive, that I was working with dissident Republicans and putting the lives of the owners, Lord Magan and his family, at risk because I mentioned that his Irish-born father had been a member of MI5. I re-read the piece and felt that I had been honest and fair, and had praised Lord Magan for restoring the place so lovingly.

I thought I had in some way done him a disservice and was seriously considering abandoning the project. That was, until I met Eileen Little, Dublin Road, Kilkenny, on the street. Her husband's family all worked in the *Kilkenny People*. She told me to carry on and not to be daft; that no self-respecting earl would take any notice of what was written about him in the *Kilkenny People* and that it was someone closer to home who was responsible. I received a phone call from a blocked number threatening me over the Castletown Cox piece shortly after that, but Brian Keyes and I still felt we should carry on the series – which we did, without any more complaints to the police or gardaí. I thought it was important to put the matter on record. I would also like to reiterate my regard for Lord Magan, who has made a huge investment in South Kilkenny and has copper-fastened the future of a most beautiful architectural and historical gem.

A few months later, a chance meeting with Mary Feehan, an old family friend, developed into this book, which for me has been a joy to write, although a source of pain for my family, who had to put up with me while I was at the kitchen table working on it.

I can safely say that I have never enjoyed anything like doing this book during my journalistic career, and meeting so many wonderful people along the way was the highlight. One person stands out – maybe it's because he passed away a few months later that I remember him so vividly and with such warmth. Sean Power was born literally yards from one of the great heritage sites in this country, Knockroe and its passage tomb, which is at the centre of an archaeological archipelago. He never left it and on the day I met him he recalled all the people who had come to marvel at the tomb. He was genuine, honest, true and yet of simple tastes, as if the material world meant little to him. He smiled when he spoke about the druids who came there on 21 December for the winter solstice and spoke with warmth about them, not disdain. He explained that we all have to live together and get on. Asked if he regretted never leaving Knockroe, he answered, 'What regrets could I have?', as he spread his arms wide indicating the wonderful landscape with the River Linuane below him forming the border between Kilkenny and Tipperary. I will never forget his wonderfully chiselled face, his clear, untainted eye and his honest stare.

I hope you have as much fun reading this book as I had writing it.

Ballyspellan Spa

Peering in at this site from the public road, with the morning sun in your eyes, all you can see is a little stone hut with the remains of stone buildings to the front, surrounded by 'Connemaresque' stone walls. Behind, there is a plantation of fir trees.[1] This is all that is left of a place once celebrated throughout the English-speaking world thanks to the 'magical' properties of the water that flows there. Throw in a link to one of Ireland's most enduring authors, Dean Jonathan Swift (author of *Gulliver's Travels*), along with the mystery of a priceless piece of jewellery found nearby, and you get a place of immense interest that formed part of the background to the best-selling nineteenth-century novel *The Evil Eye*.

The area where Ballyspellan Spa was built was clearly in use long before the spa itself was constructed. In September 1806 a 'peasant' turning over ground in a field on Ballyspellan Hill, on the farm of Charles Byrne Esq. which was on the estate of Lord Ashbrook, saw something metal. On closer examination he found a silver brooch.

---

1 The spa is located about sixteen miles from Kilkenny city and to get to it you pass through Freshford village and on for Johnstown, resisting the temptation to turn left at Minister's Cross.

16

He took it to Mr Byrne, who brought it to the Kilkenny Archaeological Society, who sent it to Dublin to what is now the National Museum. The bossed, penannular brooch is made of hammered silver and is Viking in origin. It was created around AD 900. Each half of the flat sunken area of the terminal has openwork plates with animal designs, separated by incised grooved bands connecting with five domed bosses. The bosses, which hold the openwork plates in position, are highlighted by ribbed wire rings and riveted to the brooch. The junction of the ring and terminal on both sides is decorated with an incised biting animal head. On the back of the brooch four Irish names are scratched in Ogham characters. Such is the quality and beauty of the Ballyspellan Brooch that Prince Albert presented a replica of it to Queen Victoria at Christmas 1849, having acquired it during the royal visit to Dublin in August 1849.

However, Ballyspellan is most famous for its spa. From the early part of the eighteenth century, it was receiving wealthy visitors on a regular basis, especially during the summer months. Ballyspellan was the place to go if you had a medical complaint and the money to travel. It was spoken of in the same breath as the spas at Kirby, Westmoreland, England, and at Pyrmont, Germany. People came from all over Ireland and Britain, many of them retired army and navy personnel. Whatever you had, Ballyspellan Spa was the answer.

When I look at the old adverts, they remind me of the

latest elixirs being offered by pharmaceutical companies today, promising you immunity from everything bad known to man, full of vital vitamins and other stuff. As much as things change, they stay the same. Dr Rutty, a well-known writer on mineral waters in the late 1700s, claimed that drinking the water from the spa cured pox, itch, boils, troubled minds and a variety of diseases, including 'debilitated habits of the stomach in the intestines and the lungs'. He observed the water's impact on dropsies, eruptions and blotches in the skin in a case of leprosy, and claimed that it worked wonders on obstructions of the liver and jaundice.

The claims made by 'experts' about the miracle powers of the water are hard to believe. Yet this quote from *Faulkner's Dublin Journal*, 25 May 1742, shows how popular the spa was: 'To all who have mind to drink at the famous Ballyspellan Spa in the County Kilkenny. There is good fox and hare hunting, horse racing, dancing and hurling for the pleasure of the quality at the Spa.' It provided income for a large number of families in the area, kept one local hotel in business and provided a good bit of business for two others in nearby Johnstown village.

Imagine every young person within five to ten miles descending on the spa every Sunday afternoon during the summer months, when there would be Gaelic football and hurling played, dancing and general fun. It was so famous in its day that an outrageous poem celebrating it was composed by Thomas Sheridan in 1728, although Dean

Swift penned a cutting answer to this; both of them had visited the spa that year. The two poems are included at the end of this chapter.

After the Great Famine the spa went into serious decline. In 1860, in *The Evil Eye*, William Carleton described the type of people who used to visit the spa, and the condition it was in at the time of writing, mentioning the poems as he does so:

> The society at Ballyspellan was, as the society in such places usually is, very much mixed and heterogeneous. Many gentry were there – gentlemen attempting to repair constitutions broken down by dissipation and profligacy; and ladies afflicted with a disease peculiar, in those days, to both sexes, called the spleen – a malady which, under that name, has long since disappeared, and is now known by the title of nervous affection. There was a large public room, in imitation of the more celebrated English watering-places, where the more respectable portion of the company met and became acquainted, and where, also, balls and dinners were occasionally held. Not a wreck of this edifice is now standing, although, down to the days of Swift and Delany, it possessed considerable celebrity, as is evident from the ingenious verses written by his friend to the Dean upon this subject.

The site of the spa is located about sixteen miles from Kilkenny city. There is very little of note on the way there from the spa's golden era, except for the house on the corner of the by-road up to it, the lovely ivy-clad two-storey residence that was once called Rochford's Hotel and was built in the early 1800s in response to increasing numbers going to Ballyspellan. It is now better known as the place where Irish tenor, medical doctor, bonesetter and double amputee Dr Ronan Tynan was born.

Ballyspellan Spa is, alas, no more, but the water that made it famous still flows into the well house. This *aqua pura* rises in the limestone-rich Clomantagh Hills and makes its way to Ballyspellan through fissured rock until it comes to the brow of the hill and drops down through brittle slate. When you arrive at the site, you climb the gate and walk the 150 yards to a little arched doorway. Inside is the actual spring that fed the spa and you are immediately struck by the way everything has been reddened by the iron-rich liquid. As off-putting as it looks, one taste and you are immediately hit by a heartening sensation. I don't know if my taste buds picked it out or if it was just my imagination, but it did taste really refreshing, slightly acidic and a little carbonated. Is it the fact that you are drinking cool water from an uncontaminated source, up in the hills, where there is no one to bother you except the native wildlife and the cattle lowing a few fields away? Or is it the memory of what went on here in the distant past and the fact that in the *Kilkenny Moderator* of May 1874 it was said that the spa water cured a man with 'a fatal illness'? That claim was made in the form of a letter, which was part of an attempt to rejuvenate the spa. A series of meetings were held in Johnstown and the entire spa area was cleaned and whitewashed; spa water was sold by the glass at that time for 4d per glass. Sadly the required infrastructure wasn't there and the money wasn't available to modernise the place, so it continued to decline.

Today, all that is left of the once thriving Spa is a bleak and barren remnant.

Here is the poem by Thomas Sheridan (note the different spelling of the name):

ON BALLYSPELLIN

All you that wou'd refine your Blood
As pure as fam'd Llewellyn
By Waters clear, come ev'ry Year
To drink at Ballyspellin.

Tho' Pox or Itch, your Skins enrich
With Rubies past and telling,
T'will clear your skin before you've been
A month at Ballyspellin.

If Lady's cheek be green as leek
When she comes from her Dwelling
The kindling Rose within it glows
When she's at Ballyspellin.

The sooty Brown, who comes to town
Grows here as fair as Helen

Then back she goes to kill the Beaux
By Dint of Ballyspellin ...

We Men Submit as they think fit,
And here is no rebelling:
The reason's plain, the Ladies reign
They're Queens at Ballyspellin.

By matchless Charms, unconquer'd Arms
They have the Pow'r of quelling
Such desperate Foes as dare oppose
Their Power at Ballyspellin.

Cold Water turns to Fire, and burns
I know, because I fell in
A Stream which came from one bright Dame
Who drank at Ballyspellin ...

No Politics, no subtle Tricks
No Man his country selling,
We eat, we drink, we never think
Of these at Ballyspellin.

The troubled Mind, the puft with Wind
Do all come here Pell-Mell in:
And, they are sure, to work their Cure
By drinking Ballyspellin.

If dropsy fills you to the Gills
From Chin to Toe tho' swelling
Pour in, pour out, you cannot doubt
A Cure at Ballyspellin.

Death Throws no Darts through all these Parts,
No Sextons here are knelling;
Come, judge and try, you'll never die,
But live at Ballyspellin.

Except you feel Darts tipt with Steel
Which here are ev're Belle in;
When from their Eyes sweet Ruin Flies,
We die at Ballyspellin.

Good Cheer, sweet Air, much Joy, no Care
Your Sight, your Taste, your Smelling
Your Ears, your Touch, transporteth much
Each Day at Ballyspellin.

Within this Ground we all sleep sound,
No noisy Dogs a-yelling:
Except you wake, for Celia's Sake
All Night at Ballyspellin.

Here all you see, both he and she,
No Lady keeps her Cell in;

But all partake the Mirth we make
Who drink at Ballyspellin.

My Rhimes are gone, I think I've none
Unless I should bring Hell in;
But since I am here to Heav'n so near
I can't at Ballyspellin!

And here is Swift's response:

Dare you dispute, you Sawcy Brute,
And think there's no refelling
Your scurvey Lays, and senseless praise,
You give to Ballyspellin?

Howe'er you flounce, I here pronounce
Your Med'cine is repelling;
Your water's mud, and sowrs the Blood
When drunk at Ballyspellin.

Those pocky Drabs, to cure their scabs
You thither are compelling,
Will back be sent, worse than they went
From nasty Ballyspellin.

Lewellin! Why? As well may I
Name honest Doctor Pelling;
So Hard sometimes you tug for Rimes
To bring in Ballyspellin.

No subject fit to try your wit
When you went Colonelling:
But dull intrigues twixt Jades and Teagues
That met at Ballyspellin.

Our lasses fair, say what you dare,
Who sowins make with Shelling,
At Market-hill, more beaus can kill
Than yours at Ballyspellin.

Would I was whipt, when Sheelah stript
To wash herself our Well in,
A Bum so white ne're came in sight
At Paltry Ballyspellin.

Your Mawkins there smocks hempen wear;
For Holland, not an ell in,
No, not a rag, whate'er you brag
Is found at Ballyspellin.

But, Tom will prate at any rate
All other Nymphs expelling;
Because he gets a few Grisettes
At lowsey Ballyspellin.

There's bonny Jane, in yonder lane
Just o'er against the Bell Inn;
Where can you meet a lass so sweet
Round all your Ballyspellin?

We have a girl deserves an Earl
She came from Enniskellin,
So fair, so young, no such among
The belles of Ballyspellin.

How would you stare to see her there
The foggy mists dispelling,
That cloud the Brows of ev'ry blowse
Who lives at Ballyspellin.

Now as I live, I would not give
A stiver or a skellin,
To towse and kiss the fairest Miss
That leaks at Ballyspellin.

Whoe'er will raise such lyes as these
Deserves a good cudgelling;
Who faisly boasts of belles and Toasts
At dirty Ballyspellin.

My rhymes are gone, to all but one
Which is, our trees are felling,
As proper quite as those you write
To force in Ballyspellin.

Clomantagh Castle

S itting on top of Clomantagh Castle, Margaret Butler, a tough matriarchal figure, would, it is said, gaze down from her 'holiday home' at her vast territory and at her subjects. Having sat on the exact same spot as this Great Countess of Ormonde (d. 1552), I can see how she would have been impressed by what she owned and saw: the Slieveardagh Hills, across to Woodsgift, to the castle at Minister's Cross, to Mount Garrett-Clomantagh, to Spa Hill, with Freshford to her back.

The castle served as a retreat from Kilkenny Castle on the Nore and Grannagh Castle on the Suir where she resided with her husband, Piers Roe, Earl of Ormonde (d. 1539). From its lofty perch you can see that the landscape is dotted with hill forts, cairns, fairy forts and various minor medieval installations. Here too was a community, as can be seen by the presence of a well adjacent to the tower house of the castle, a ruined church, numerous buildings and an enclosing wall.

Clomantagh passed, with many other castles and lands, to the Earl and Countess of Ormonde's second son, Richard Butler, the 1st Viscount Mountgarret. The 3rd Lord Mountgarret was president of the Confederation of Kilkenny, and forfeited the castle and a third of the townland under the Cromwellian regime to Lieutenant Arthur St George, ancestor of the Kilrush/Callan St George family. The castle was also owned by the Shortalls of Ballylarkin, and latterly by Mr Willie White, a vet in the nearby village of Freshford.

The word 'unique' is often misused, but in the case of Clomantagh Castle it is appropriate. It is a magical place, strikingly set within a series of buildings dating from the twelfth century, including a medieval dovecote and church closer to the public road.[2] Nowhere else in Ireland can be found this fusion of an original fifteenth-century castle with an early nineteenth-century farmhouse. The castle is in perfect symmetry with the farmhouse, which stands where the old banqueting hall used to be, and it is probable that the stone from the vanished banqueting hall, which was an integral part of the castle, went into the building of the Victorian house. High up on the castle wall facing the road is a female fertility carving of a Sheela na Gig, which was probably removed from the ruined church below. The buildings have been preserved for the people of Kilkenny by the little-known, but highly effective, Irish Landmark Trust, which bought the castle from Mr White. It has to be said that the area seems to have been neglected by officialdom, and it is great that

---

2   To get there, drive from Kilkenny city to Freshford and follow the signposts for Urlingford. Three miles further on you come to Delaney's pub on the left and another mile further is Clomantagh.

there is a benevolent entity like this to maintain our heritage.

As Clomantagh was painstakingly and authentically restored, the moment you enter the castle you are hit by the intimate relationship between the two architectural styles, which gives you the feeling of floating between centuries as you step from room to room. The kitchen, which would do justice to the front page of any country-home-and-living magazine, and the main bedroom are located in the tower house, and a medieval stone turret staircase leads between the two. Warmth is generated by the stove and kept in by the centuries-old walls and roof. The Tower Room, complete with four-poster bed, has a view of Clomantagh-Mount Garrett.

The Victorian farmhouse, which is a fine example of its type, retains most of its original features, apart from the roofing material, which was changed from thatch to slate around 1850. The rooms are straight out of a TV period drama and there are exquisite touches everywhere. The Blue Room is another exquisite bedroom and the children's bedroom on two levels, with its original spy hole from the castle, will have any child dreaming of Merlin, Robin Hood, druids, knights and the Middle Ages.

At the heart of Irish Landmark's work is the principle that the structure itself is of prime importance and any interventions must respect this. Thus, the trust applies rigorous policies to its conservation work, ensuring the history, evolution, form, materials, setting, environment and original purpose of the buildings are preserved as far as possible. All the properties reflect a careful balance between the demands of conservation and conversion, which allows them to be developed without compromising the original internal spaces in the building. This is so at Clomantagh: so when you enter this realm you are part of a living history which most people know little or nothing about.

There is another aspect of Clomantagh which attracts much attention today. A canny Irishman was once asked: 'Do you believe in ghosts?' He answered: 'No, but they are there all right.' Such is the case with Clomantagh: there is 'Tom', who died in 1849 and whose surname cannot be mentioned because it might upset his relations still living close by. Another spectre, 'Sally', is regularly referred to in the visitor's book. I joined members of the Kilkenny Investigative Paranormal Society (KIPS) as they spent a night in the castle with all their electronic gizmos, which got some very strong readings. The volunteers spent hours setting up the monitors, including infrared cameras and special records capable of detecting sounds which humans can't hear. As I and members of KIPS stood in one of the bedrooms approaching midnight, the temperature dropped suddenly, the power seemed to leave my mobile phone and a gust of wind whistled past us even though the windows and door were closed.

There have been a lot of unexplained events in the castle, like the grandfather clock in the kitchen permanently set at 11.30 a.m., which one day, when manager Susan Garrett was upstairs, chimed twelve times. She got a fright. The clock has not made a move since. Susan's enthusiasm for Clomantagh is palpable and she loves showing off the house to people, but she will not stay in the kitchen at night on her own, and while there are parts of the house she feels comfortable in, there are others, well …

The thatched villages
of South Kilkenny

One of the largest collections of traditional thatched houses is set in a unique part of South Kilkenny. The farm villages of Licketstown, Glengrant, Moonveen, Luffany and Carrigeen, close to Mooncoin and tucked into a curve of the River Suir just off the N24, are beautifully constructed and linked by raised banks used as flood barriers, walkways and boundaries, which created a way of life still preserved today by a dwindling population. Here, the thatch is the signature of a self-reliant and assured people. They have existed largely unchanged for generations. Here can also be found a dialect that exists nowhere else and a form of English going back to Elizabethan times. Home to a former president of the GAA and a celebrated novelist, the thatched homes and villages are an important part of our heritage, and yet they are largely unheard of in Kilkenny city.

Although numbers are declining, there is a pride of place here that is hard to match. And the communities' continued existence is thanks to the sun-drenched, lime-rich earth where almost anything can grow. The deep,

fertile land brought a prosperity with it that kept generations of O'Keefes, Walshs, Purcells, Delahuntys and
others alive. Hard to believe that manure was so valuable
in Luffany, Moonveen, Glengrant and Licketstown in the
1850s that farmers from here bid for the right to scrape
the dung off the streets of Waterford city – there were so
few cows in this little valley where tillage, vegetables and
fruit were the main crops that the dung was needed to
fertilise the land. These people had a belief in themselves
that was anything but arrogant, and such a wonderful way
of life that they didn't need much else. They built their
villages close to the water's edge where temperatures all
through the year are a degree or two warmer than even
a mile away. The villages are like a mixture of something
out of Tolkien's *The Hobbit* and all that is good about the
Amish enclaves in America. The inhabitants of this, the
southern tip of Leinster, are a wonderful people doing
their bit to keep a part of our living heritage alive.

One of the cottages in Glengrant is the birthplace of
the great Bob O'Keeffe, a native who played hurling and
won All Ireland medals with Laois. The Leinster Senior
Championship Cup was named in his honour and he
was also a president of the Gaelic Athletic Association.
His grandniece, Mary Murphy, née O'Keeffe, and her
husband John Joe rethatched the house last year and other
outhouses that surround it. They also keep the raised bank
(double ditch) between Glengrant and Moonveen weed-
free, out of a sense of duty and as a mark of respect to

those who went before them. There are no grants: Mary and John Joe carried out the work simply because they have pride in their own place.

Mary, John Joe and Mary's sister Margaret live in the centre of Licketstown, in a lovely thatched cottage, an exquisite example of what can be done with a bit of effort. Mary remembers when over 100 people lived in the immediate area, almost all in thatched cottages, and none went hungry. In fact, the parishes of Carrigeen and Mooncoin are dotted with thatch in varying degrees of upkeep. Mikey Walsh, also of Licketstown, has built a number of thatch homes and these seem destined to endure. In other parts of the country there are fake villages with harness makers, a forge and diddly-diddle-type stalls for the tourist market, while here in South Kilkenny the real thing exists.

The thatched houses, with their painted wooden shutters, the intricate designs on the wooden fascias and other little touches, are so like those in the Basque Country that, although the links have never been investigated, I have to ask myself if the villages were influenced by the many French and Spanish ships that came up the tidal Suir. In other countries there would be books written about the detailed design of these thatched houses; thanks have to go to Joe Cashin for keeping a pictorial record of the area.

The inhabitants of these places weren't peasant farmers like in the west of Ireland; theirs was a sophisticated, social dynamic of farm villages linked by high banks, impervious to flooding. And the land is rich in archaeological gems, such as the Neolithic stone axe head found on Pat Dunphy's land a few miles away at Ballygorey that is over 6,000 years old. This is by far the most remarkable part of Kilkenny city and county: it survived the Butlers, Cromwell, plantations, famine, civil wars and the weather, and yet most people have no idea that this enclave exists. In his excellent essay on the 'Farm Villages of South Kilkenny', historian Jack Burchaell explained that the people living here were cut off from the rolling plains of the rest of South Kilkenny by sandstone and granite uplands. Blessed with great alluvial soil by the Suir, they were part of a feudal system where for hundreds of years farmers were left to farm with little interference from those who owned the land, so long as they paid their rent on time. Older people here still recall being told that their farm villages were the bread basket of Waterford city.

The River Suir is also the reason for the multitude of thatch in the area. It was the reeds growing on its banks which were used to thatch the houses, and the cot net fishermen, with their narrow, flat-bottomed boats, used to cut the reeds for the thatch: they fitted perfectly into the long, narrow craft. It was good to see local man Willie Power out on his cot going up and down the Suir on a beautiful spring day.

To get a sense of a place you must turn to its writers. The following lines are from the novel *Hanrahan's Daughter* by the Moonveen-born writer Patrick Purcell, and they give a flavour of life in this most exquisite and haunting part of the country. They were brought to my attention by Jack Burchaell:

> For the honour of the old parish, for the name of the hurling blood, for the white-washed walls of little villages by the river, beneath the hills, Clonmore to Carrigeen, Dournane to Aiglish, Moonveen to Luffany, Clogga to Knockanure, for the memory never forgotten of many hard won triumph [*sic*], for the bitterness of dark defeat, for the glory evergreen of half score All Irelands, for the name and fame of the victory to be brought home to the quiet houses by the calm river; for the proud smile the prowess of their men folk would bring to the lips of the gentle women who kept the fire burning in the far villages and glens.

Billy Sullivan and his two sisters, Mary and Jo, have rarely left Licketstown and the furthest they have travelled is to Waterford city. In their seventies and eighties now, they are still going strong in their home, which was once thatched but today has a slate roof. They use words I have never heard before, such as 'oncest' instead of once, and others rhythmical to the ear and although different, still making sense. So we have yet another reason to thank these people, as they have kept alive a dying dialect and a way of speaking that has almost been lost.

Moonveen is a Gaelic name and means the smooth bog land, but it's peat like I have never seen. It is rich in plant life and excellent for growing tillage crops or potatoes.

The temperature here is always a little above the norm and these people were canny when it came to building a home. They knew what they were doing when they faced the houses across the River Suir to County Waterford to catch the evening sun, and built them down close enough to the water's edge to get the shade from the other side and to duck the strong winds up the estuary. This is the most southerly part of the county, in the diocese of Ossory and indeed in the province of Leinster. And a converted thatch cottage, now a plain-roofed house, named Riverdale is the most southerly house in the province, facing the River Suir a field away. Fields surround it with beautiful names such as Scraitheán and An Tulán. Like Slieverue, the farm villages here were Irish-speaking up to the middle of the last century, which explains why the Gaelic names still survive.

So, if you are looking to entertain family or visitors, bring them down to Licketstown, Moonveen, Glengrant and Luffany, and let them see Ireland's past, our heritage, and be amazed at the particular style of architecture in the thatched house, before these disappear from our landscape completely.

Woodstock

W oodstock, near the village of Inistioge, is like
Neverland. It's as if Tinker Bell scattered fairy
dust along this tree-mendous trail of Titan-like redwoods,
hooky monkey-puzzle trees, weeping Irish beech and
sacred Japanese Arborvitae. In the face of such glory,
'arboretum' seems like such a non-word and 'forest' so
plain. Woodstock is much more than the sum of its parts
– it never leaves you: the creaking of the thick torsos in the
summer breeze; the scent of wild woodbine beneath them
in autumn; the sound of river water; the birds …

Wonderfully haunting, with magical forest walks and
two breathtaking avenues – one of noble fir and the other
of monkey-puzzles – Woodstock is bordered by the River
Nore and a place where red squirrels thrive. Set here is
the saga of the great Tighe family, who have left us with
so much to enrich our lives. Unexplained deaths, murder,
intrigue and financial difficulties hit them hard. But the
love of gardening also began with the Tighes. The men of
the family were high-ranking British officers who travelled throughout the British Empire, and their quest for
something different led to their collection of exotic trees
from faraway places for their arboretum at Woodstock.

This is also where a woman of substance brought about a Renaissance-like revival and was the beneficiary of the first ecumenical funeral in Ireland. Lady Louisa Tighe, who died in 1900, was the real guiding force behind this place of beauty, grace, reputation and, most of all, blessed trees. Her godfather was the Duke of Wellington of Waterloo fame, her father a heavy-drinking duellist. In his excellent book, *Abandoned Ireland*, Tarquin Blake notes that Lady Louisa was remarkable in that she was the only woman besides the queen of England who had the power to pardon criminals – even at the foot of the gallows:

> She apparently exercised this right twice a year with great care and wisdom. In one case Lady Louisa banished a criminal from Ireland. Her steward had confessed to the crimes of stealing the Richmond black diamond and the Duke of Richmond's watch. His only punishment was that he was ordered to leave the country.

Lady Louisa supervised everything and worked with the head gardeners, Pierce Butler and Charles McDonald, to make Woodstock the envy of all others. When the best-known collectors of rare specimens in Victorian times, the Menzies, were offered the seeds of the monkey-puzzle tree to eat at a dinner party hosted by the governor of Chile, their mouths opened in awe, not hunger, and they put them straight into their pockets. The seeds that form part of the staple diet of the red squirrels at Woodstock are from the descendents of the trees grown by the Tighes from these original seeds provided by the Menzies.

Woodstock also has a strong association with a wonderful pair of unconventional, and possibly lesbian, Victorian women (the Ladies of Llangollen). It is said that these bored women dressed up as milking-parlour maids in a game at the 'Baths', where they could not be seen except by those seated on a number of stones, from where (we presume) the menfolk watched them. One of the seats also had a little waterfall which ran over the person sitting. It could well be a scene out of Hardy's *Tess of the d'Urbervilles*.

For some, Woodstock is epitomised by the Turner-designed conservatory where the toffs enjoyed afternoon tea. For others it is characterised by the rounded dovecote, where the pigeons were kept and which provided six-week-old chicks for the dining-room table to the pampered residents of the big house. Then there is the exquisite walled garden, once heated by giant fires which warmed specially placed bricks that released heat to the glasshouses growing such exotics as melons. It is strange to think that 150 years ago young boys stoked the fires behind the walled garden all night to keep them burning, while sleeping overhead and sharing their lodgings with spailpíns and journeymen gardeners who came to marvel and to learn. The long-since quenched fires explain the chimney on the corner of the west side of the walled garden. There is still a microclimate at play in the walled

garden and here everything was grown, from flowers for
the displays to the spuds and the herbs.

At the epicentre of this world is the burned-out shell of
Woodstock House, sealed off for reasons of safety. There
are plans to place a structure inside to explain the history of
the place, which was built in 1747. Three storeys high and
greatly extended in 1804 it was, we know from paintings,
rather amazing. In 1921 during the War of Independence
it was occupied by the Black and Tans, which left a bad
taste, and when the Civil War followed the Free State
army took it over. The Republicans, the IRA, burned it
down on 1 July 1922 having sent the Free State troops
– their former brothers in arms and then sworn enemies
– out on a wild-goose chase. The burning of the big house
here summed up the hatred and bitterness in the country
during the Civil War.

For their inspired vision in buying and preserving
this place, having been spurred on by former Fine Gael
Councillor Andy Cotterell and the rest of those involved
in a FÁS course there, Kilkenny County Council should
take a bow. County manager Paddy Donnelly was always
innovative, as was the newly appointed county engineer
of the time, Don O'Sullivan, while the county secretary
back then, Philip O'Neill, helped the local people any
way he could. It has borne fruit. Fifty acres were sold to
the council for a nominal £100 by Mr Anthony Tighe of
Northants in England around 1998–99; the rest of the
estate has been leased out to Coillte, the state forestry,

much of it now comprising commercial plantations, felled every twenty-five years or so.

Head gardener John Delaney, from Ballyragget, explained the essence of the place to me: 'It's the trees.' And as he spoke, looking down the walled garden, with the fog lifting over Woodstock, landscape architect Claire Goodwin nodded her head in agreement. Thanks to the tender loving care of John and his team, the walled garden still looks magnificent and is worth the price of admission on its own. The other gardeners – Tommy Smyth, Matt Drea, Patrick McGrath, John Bennett and Liam Curran – also do a fantastic job: to think there are thirty acres of grass to be mowed before you do anything else! It is a labour of love and a true vocation. They understand they are the trustees of the best tree-garden in Europe, a fact agreed by experts the world over. The work at Woodstock never stops and you have to keep on top of it or it will go feral again. The magnificence of the trees is at the heart of Woodstock. It conjures up the image of far-flung ships bringing back priceless seeds, saplings and plants from exotic places for re-planting at Woodstock under the watchful eye of Lady Louisa.

As you walk around the pleasure lawns, past the playground on the left, the popular and Latin names are written in little plaques at the bottom of each tree. If you take your time you can imagine the Tighes in the big house coming out on the front lawn for a game of croquet and checking the health of the latest specimen brought back from Mexico or the Russian Steppes. Or think of the path in the walled garden, which was made wide enough to allow two women in the voluminous dresses of the day to pass, with tall borders on each side to ensure they did not see where the vegetables were grown.

In her delightful book *The 100 Best Gardens in Ireland*, Shirley Lanigan shares her enthusiasm for Woodstock with the readers: 'All over the pleasure grounds, clearances have revealed gardens not seen properly for nearly a century; the yew walk and kitchen gardens, only barely discernible until lately.' There are a number of walks available around the gardens, with the longest doing the full circle from Woodstock down to the river passing close to the Red House, built as a shooting lodge by the Tighes. In this idyllic spot, people tied their boats directly below. As you get to within striking distance of the village, on your left, high up the fir-covered slope, is Mount Sandford Castle, a folly built in 1769. It has the best views of the river and the village.

The Ice House is also situated along the walk. It was here that ice was stored, and, when needed, chunks were carved out and carried up to the big house. It is now home to a roost of Daubenton's bats. Walk in, the bats won't bother you.

The American redwoods, which are around 150 years old and are native to a small area of California where John Steinbeck set many of his novels, should keep growing for hundreds of years to come, and will eventually dwarf every other thing living at Woodstock. They might even climb as high as nearby Mount Alto, from where fresh-water streams feed the estate.

My favourite tree is the Japanese Arborvitae (the tree of life, *Thuja standishii*) between the winter garden and the walled garden – a woman walking at Woodstock in January 2012, as an Operation Transformation event was being held, said she saw some visitors bowing in courtesy to it.

Enhancing Woodstock never ends. All the original garden furniture was sold at auction in the 1950s. However, much of it has now been replaced and, by using old photos, this has been done authentically. The most important piece of this jigsaw is the conservatory, which was completely dismantled and sold for scrap. All that was left were the stone bases, and even these had been smashed by vandals, but the Powers of New Ross have expertly carried out its restoration to the highest standard. One of the most memorable views at Woodstock is from behind the seat facing the conservatory with the terraced garden in between. The gardeners excavated the area and found traces of the old garden, including the original cinders marking circular borders – and that is what you see today.

If you visit Woodstock, you must also go to the village of Inistioge and explore the Church of Ireland chapel in the corner of the village square and, more importantly, the old abbey and graveyard behind, which has been scrupulously cleaned up by local people. There is a memorial here to the poet Mary Tighe, who died at Woodstock in 1810, while the tombs of both Lady Louisa and her husband, William, are in the tower of the old abbey, which has been sealed. The tower looks like it could collapse at any moment, but it is still worth visiting.

Lady Louisa's hand can be seen here as well: she erected the fountain in the middle of the square in 1879 in memory of William. When she died, the local Catholic clergy and the Church of Ireland bishop were present at her funeral, the Union Jack was placed on her coffin and Inistioge came to a standstill.

Jerpoint Abbey

T o understand the true importance of Jerpoint
Abbey, Thomastown (situated after a bend on the
road, along the old national primary route to Waterford
(N9)), you must go back to when it was at the height of
its powers before the dissolution of the monasteries in
the 1540s. As you walk around the cloister (the square-
shaped covered walk) with the green 'garth' in the centre,
you should try to imagine the White Monks, their heads
bearing the shaved tonsure of their order as they trod the
cloister walkways, praying or singing in Gregorian chant.
As they walked by the beautifully designed and simple
structure that has passed down to us, it would have been
difficult for them not to be touched by the different
images that confronted them.

These images, carved in stone, include St Anthony of
Egypt, the 4th Earl of Ormonde, a manticore (a mythical
creature with a lion's body, a human head and a scorpion's
tail), a wyvern (a winged creature with a dragon's head,
lizard's body, two legs and a barbed tail), a man apparently
suffering from a stomach upset, knights and images of
both St Catherine of Alexandria and St Margaret of
Antioch. Interestingly both of these female figures are

represented three times in Jerpoint, along with a carving of St Mary, and echo some drawings found on medieval manuscripts.

Jerpoint was very much an all-male, hierarchical system with the lower-class lay brothers not allowed into the cloister and living in a separate area outside the inner sanctum. And let's put one thing to rest. St Nicholas (now commonly known as Santa Claus) was not buried here by knights coming back from the crusades. Folklore has it that his remains, or a piece of his body, or a relic associated with him lie in the abbey, and although it's a lovely, romantic tale, it has no basis in truth and no written record to support it. But that does not mean that there is no link to St Nicholas in the area. He is strongly associated with the church named after him not far from the abbey and close to the lost village of Jerpoint. This church does have a certain aura and, who knows, the remains of St Nicholas may have ended up there.

The village of Jerpoint, which grew beside the abbey, declined dramatically in the seventeenth century, probably as a result of the earlier dissolution of the monasteries and the subsequent removal of the monks from the abbey. It has now been lovingly and wonderfully unearthed and brought to life by Joe O'Connell.

On first seeing the abbey itself, one commentator described 'the dark, biscuit-coloured tower of Jerpoint Abbey'. What an apt description – and that colour is in part due to the Dundry stone used in its construction.

The fact that it has survived wars and natural calamities to remain relatively intact is amazing. There are no rich tapestries, no priceless antiques and no portraits of inbred toffs with long noses, but within the abbey's walls you can touch history and appreciate the lifestyle of those who lived and died here.

Receiving a five-star tour from one of the most eminent scholars on the Cistercians in Ireland, Dr Breda Lynch, helps one to appreciate Jerpoint. *A Monastic Landscape: The Cistercians in Medieval Ireland* is a detailed study of various aspects of the Cistercian order in medieval Leinster, including Jerpoint, by the Slieverue-born academic. It focuses on the lands held by the great Cistercian monasteries of Leinster, including the great houses of Mellifont, Baltinglass, Jerpoint, Duiske, Tintern and Dunbrody, in the province. As we walked together up the wooden stairs to where the monks' dormitory was, because the roof has long since been removed, we could see the Kilkenny–Waterford railway line where, in times past, trains stopped and people got off to view the abbey. In the fields below the first floor we could make out the outlines of the various outbuildings and defences as well as the remains of the drainage system, which may have included a system of reed beds (eco-friendly monks!).

The meagre sleeping quarters remind you once again of the austerity of the lives of the monks. Their day started at two o'clock every morning when they would have walked down the stairs from the dormitory to the ground floor and into the church. There they sang in Gregorian chant, the first of the nine prayerful periods, in the hope of getting another poor soul stuck in limbo into heaven. I'm not sure there would be many takers today for the life of a monk in an enclosed order.

The Cistercians who founded Jerpoint were originally from Citeaux, France, and were followers of the Rule of St Benedict, which revolved around three basic principles: peace, prayer and work. To see them through each long day they were allowed one pound of coarse bread and two dishes of boiled vegetables. It gets a little better: they were also allowed eight pints of abbey-made beer every day. This beer was thick and had to be strained before drinking. It was lighter than today's Smithwick's, but it was this beer that gave them the energy, we are led to believe, to keep going. It was claimed that back then there was less chance of getting sick from the beer than there was from drinking the water. The monks were banned from eating any four-legged animal, but they could feed on chicken, fowl and fish. Standing in front of the calefactory (again without a roof), Dr Lynch explained that a fire was lit in this communal sitting room on All Soul's Day and quenched on Good Friday. This was the only heat in the entire complex.

And here, four times a year, the poor monks were cut and drained of up to four pints of blood. Yes, sixteen pints a year. There was even a special 'monastic blood pit' at many monasteries like Jerpoint. In medieval and early modern times it was erroneously thought that 'letting blood' was good for all sorts of ailments and it was common practice across the medieval world.

The abbey was founded around 1170, and records show that by 1228 there were thirty-six monks and fifty brothers living there. By the fifteenth century it had lost some of its austerity, and the monuments to lay people and the secular wall paintings, still to be seen inside the abbey, are a testament to that. When the monastery was handed over to the Butlers of Ormonde in 1540, the abbot, Oliver Grace, surrendered a castle, several water mills, cottages, weirs and fisheries, and around 14,500 acres.

Of course what we're left with today only tells half the story. There would have been outer defences where craftspeople plied their trades and where the vegetable rows, herb gardens, orchards, granary and other intricate features of everyday life were situated. The inside and outside walls of the main body of the abbey were not what we see today. They were plastered and whitewashed and then false masonry joints added to make it look more authentic – it all seems a bit flash to us for an abbey, but was considered normal in those days. The Cistercians were also very hospitable and the abbey acted as an inn or hostel for travellers. Jerpoint was constantly trying to outdo its sister monastery Duiske, in Graignamanagh, and records show that the occupants of each abbey fought for years over control of the daughter house in Kilkenny.

The oldest surviving part of the abbey is the chancel

(the space around the altar in the sanctuary) and the original altar was, it is said, found hidden in the parish church of Thomastown and returned after the changes introduced by the Second Vatican Council. One of the more fascinating parts of Jerpoint is in the north transept, which with the chancel and the south transept formed the cruciform shape that is a feature of all abbeys. This dates from the fifteenth century, although it was designed in the earlier, Romanesque style. In a chapel in the north transept is a beautiful set of carvings known as The Weepers, sculpted, it is thought, by the famous O'Tunney family from Callan, as was the tomb below it.

Abbeys weren't democratic institutions and the abbot was an all-powerful prince-type figure, presiding over the meetings of the monks in the chapter house. The room has been restored and is now complete with underground heating and lots of modern technical gizmos, which in no way interfere with the fabric of the interior. It is a long, undivided space covered with a barrel vault and, although the monks observed a vow of silence the rest of the time, here every day, we are told, they were allowed to talk. The rules of St Benedict would be read out, any problems discussed and, more importantly, any punishments meted out.

Just off the chancel, the original sacristy survives, which also served as a library in medieval times. It is now used for storage while on the other side of the chapter house is the prior's office, which again has been painstakingly restored and displays various pieces of masonry, with a note on each one explaining its significance. The abbot had a separate residence from the abbey, presumably with all the trappings of luxury you would expect from a man in control of thousands of acres, water mills, fisheries, eel traps, etc. – the list goes on and on.

Jerpoint Abbey still has a huge significance and strong resonance with the surrounding community. Although there have been no funerals in the abbey precincts for the last few years, local families are still entitled to be interred here.[3] If you are from the Jerpoint area, like the retired Catholic Bishop of Ossory, Dr Laurence Forristal, you will have great memories of the place, and people from the area have a great respect for, and pride in, the abbey and the holy men who made it. Maybe that's why it has lasted so long – the reverence of the community for it and their keenness to share it with others.

---

3   The guides at Jerpoint are in possession of a map from early in the twentieth century, which shows the various family plots dotted around the abbey. The supervisor, Dr Breda Lynch, would be interested in discussing it with anyone who thinks they might be able to name some of the plots.

Kilfane

The word Kilfane, for me, conjures up images of a long-dead knight, immortalised in stone; of a Shangri-La-type glen and waterfall; and a mansion, owned by the family who look after the rights to Margaret Mitchell's epic novel, *Gone with the Wind*. Located on the outskirts of Thomastown, close to the Long Man pub and restaurant, Kilfane glen is the ideal place to while away an afternoon, exploring the walks, waterfall and the effigy of the Long Man of Kilfane. The glen and waterfall are like a fantasy land – there is even a cottage *orné* or decorated cottage, which dates back to a movement of Romantic, rustic, stylised cottages from the late eighteenth and early nineteenth centuries, and this is exactly where you would expect to find a fairytale character living.

Kilfane comes from the Irish *Cill Pháin* – the Church of Saint Paan – who, according to Canon Carrigan's history of the diocese of Ossory, was associated with the area in the early period of Christianity. Kilfane House was once the home of Sir John Power, the man responsible for Kilfane glen, waterfall and cottage. The most famous story about the house is recounted by the late Dr Walter Walsh in the local historical journal, *In the Shadow of the Steeple*:

A stranger had joined in with the hunt one day and made such a good impression on Sir John Power he invited him back to Kilfane House that evening to join in the festivities. The day was now drawing to a close, the fire was dying down and the card game was in progress. At about the dead hour of night one of the gentlemen's cards fell on the floor and on his attempting to retrieve it, he noticed that the card which fell from his hand was 'the Joker' and furthermore, the stranger who had joined them earlier that day had a cloven hoof.

Sir John, on being told of the matter, became very alarmed and sent for the local Minister who arrived and later requested that the parish priest of Thomastown, Fr Cody, be called to assist him. When he came he placed items of his apparel in each corner of the drawing room and began the exorcism. Thereupon the stranger, like a flash of lightning, went up through the ceiling and out through the domed skylight of the small corridor upstairs.

At the time, a large candelabrum hung in the main hall of the house and Sir John is said to have presented it to Fr Cody and it hung in the parish church in Thomastown but was eventually sold to help pay for renovations. Later it was presented to the Victoria and Albert Museum, Kensington, London, where it hangs in a room on the fourth floor with an inscription nearby.

But it is the waterfall that draws you. As Tennyson said, 'the wild cataract leaps in glory', and so it does here. If you stand beneath the thirty-foot cascade, the spray washes over you, refreshing the pores, even in the middle of December. Tennyson was writing about Killarney and, in some ways, Kilfane is like a mini-Muckross or Torc, such is the natural beauty of the place. Because it became overgrown with rhododendrons and laurels over 200 years, well away from subsequent nineteenth- and early twentieth-century domestic and agricultural activities, it was not meddled with, so that this very compact and most articulate and romantic place could be rescued and conserved in an absolutely strict and authentic manner by Nicky and Susan Mosse of Bennettsbridge.

Working from nothing more than a print of the grounds from 1805, Susan and Nicky Mosse have recreated this timeless wonder in painstaking fashion. When they first saw the picture, they wondered if it was painted from the imagination of the artist, but after a while, as the area was cut back, many of the original features that it records were revealed. The print proved to be a historical record and gave the Mosses a blueprint from which to work. To ensure that everything was done to the highest standard, the Mosses employed the late Sybil Connolly to design the interior of the little thatched cottage that belongs in a fairytale like Goldilocks and the Three Bears. The walks around the glen and gardens are charming and the moss-draped trees, playful streams and natural fauna all combine to provide the visitor with a blissful experience. There are wild animals here as well and the red squirrel is rumoured to be here thanks to the pine martens, which are killing off the larger, imported grey squirrels.

Kilfane was originally designed under the influence of

Rousseau and the Romantic movement. A central element in this new type of garden were artificial waterfalls and cascades, constructed to 'create and heighten a series of picturesque scenes which might embody the perfect romantic attitude and transport the soul in a sweet and tender melancholy', according to the Kilfane website. I am glad to say that the place has had the opposite impact on the people I know who have gone there to enjoy the sound of the waterfall and receive a measure of tranquillity. The impact lingers with you.

The waterfall was built by diverting water from a stream before it enters a ravine and conducting it along a small canal or feeder channel over a mile in length, from which it emerges to fall over a rocky cliff thirty feet high. From the pool at the base of the cliff, a small watercourse runs to rejoin the main stream close by, which at this point flows through a grassy lawn at the centre of the glen. Adjoining the waterfall a few yards to the west, a rustic grotto was created at the base of the cliff.

It would seem that every person who visits the water-fall finds solace there. It might not be suitable for younger children – prams or buggies – but for older children it is a treasure trove of memorable possibilities.

On the opposite side of the main stream, facing the grotto and waterfall, sits the thatched summerhouse or cottage home, a resting place for visitors. Surrounded by a grassy clearing, the cottage allows the fullest contemplation and enjoyment of the place. There is a series of meandering paths by the stream and up the steep sloping side of the ravine which should be explored: the creation of a series of charming tableaux adds to the enchantment. Rustic seats, bridges across the water and a fountain at the foot of the cliff provide the wow factor.

The formal gardens are a must for those with green fingers. To quote the excellent Shirley Lanigan from her wonderful book, *The 100 Best Gardens in Ireland*:

> Apart from the old wood garden, several new gardens were created, including a blue orchard. At its centre, crab apples have been grown in a circle and under-planted with grape hyacinths or muscari and bluebells. The facing wall backs a blue bed of agapanthus, monkshood, delphinium and aubrietia. The formal pond looks down on the all-white moon garden.

Shirley has said that Kilfane is her favourite woodland garden in Ireland.

The occupants of Kilfane House have always had a huge impact on the surrounding area, and the current owners, Louise and Thomas 'Hal' Clarke, sponsor a number of events in the neighbourhood. The Clarkes bought Kilfane House and the eighty-acre estate in 1969. Hal is a former counsel to a number of US presidents and was the lawyer who represented the trust controlling the rights to the book *Gone with the Wind* and the film of the same name. This work is continued by his family. Louise just happened to be a next-door neighbour of the author of *Gone with the Wind*, Margaret Mitchell, back in Atlanta, Georgia, where the book is set, and was friends with her. For the last forty years the devoted couple have made Kilfane House their summer residence, where their return, like that of the swallows, is eagerly anticipated by their many friends.

Kilfane Church, a mile down the road from the glen and waterfall, is also worth exploring. We learn from Tullaherin Heritage Society that the original church on this site was founded by St Paan around the time of St Patrick. The present building, with its adjoining Norman tower house, dates from the fourteenth or fifteenth century. It features a number of interesting items, including traces of the original consecration crosses (in red) on the wall near the west doorway and on the north and south walls, and the three original ogee-headed doorways – two in the south wall and one in the north wall near the sacristy door. The most remarkable feature is undoubtedly the famous effigy of An Cantwell Fada dating from the mid-thirteenth to early fourteenth centuries. This depicts a Norman knight in full armour. The entire body is covered in a suit of chain mail over which is draped a loose cloth surcoat. The shield, which features the Cantwell coat of arms, is held in the left hand. The sword is partly hidden behind his legs. Around the ankles are strapped rowel spurs, an important feature in dating the sculpture. The legs are crossed, which is thought to signify that the subject took part in the crusades. The skilful carving of the features, combined with its early date of execution and excellent state of preservation, makes An Cantwell Fada a unique treasure amongst Ireland's medieval antiquities. Across the road is the centuries-old Church of Ireland building, which is still used for worship today.

Open during the summer months, Kilfane is an absolutely mesmerising place, and not at all what you would expect when you enter from the narrow road. There are many wonderful experiences to be had there, so if you want to spend an adventurous afternoon or indeed a whole day, then Kilfane is well worth a visit.

Danesfort Turret

It is only when you are on top of the slightly unstable two-storey turret at Danesfort that you realise its close connection to Freestone Hill, Clara, an important prehistoric site that is discussed later in the book. Over the millennia the hill on which Danesfort Turret sits had been used by many different tribes and races. Although the turret, built in the latter half of the 1700s, has dominated the landscape for the last four generations, it was predated by a ring fort on the exact same spot, dating back thousands of years to before the coming of Christianity. A community lived here, with the commanding views on all sides enhancing their security. However, it is the story of what happened here around the 1870s, to an upper-class Kilkenny family who had been given the royal concession to hold fairs in Bennettsbridge twice a year and who built the turret, that sticks in your head.

The Wemys family used the (in)famous landmark on the old Kilkenny–Waterford road as a hunting folly or party house. We know from the descendants of workers who came from Britain to work for the family that, on summer evenings, the Wemys women and female guests would walk the short distance from Danesfort House to

the octagonal structure that overlooks the new Dublin–
Waterford motorway (and is on the right as you drive to
Waterford on the old main road) to join their menfolk.
While the ladies remained downstairs in the octagonal
building, the Wemys men and their mates would 'retire'
upstairs for brandy and cigars. After a good few 'shots',
they would take down the rifles hanging on the walls and
open the windows while their servants would herd the deer
on the estate past the hunting den for them to shoot at.
This involved no small amount of risk for the unfortunate
workmen, who would put the castrated and domesticated
animals between themselves and their masters. While no
one was killed, a few unfortunate local people did receive
minor wounds from shotgun pellets!

Much of what we now know about Danesfort and its
history is due to publisher, writer, historian, researcher and
bookseller Frank McEvoy. It is only now, after his death,
that we are beginning to appreciate the huge legacy he has
left us. His painstaking investigations into the turret and
former Danesfort House are in a class all of their own,
and of course, there is his detective work on tracing the
sculpture at Danesfort House, the Wemys involvement in
the theft of this priceless bronze piece and how it came to
be at the turret in the first place.

The sculpture of the Catholic King of England, James
II, which stood for decades in Walsh's field close to the
turret, was originally located in a Dublin park. A leading
authority on seventeenth- and eighteenth-century art

considered the statue, known locally as 'The Metal Man', to be the work of a Dutch artist and the finest bronze statue in England or Ireland. One night in the mid-1800s, well-heeled pranksters (possibly inebriated) with nothing better to do made a wager with each other that one of them could remove it from the park without being noticed and have it shipped from Waterford to England. The young man chosen to attempt the task was a Wemys from Danesfort House. He and some accomplices loaded the statue onto a cart and brought it through Kilkenny on their way to Waterford city. Hearing a 'posse' behind them they quickened their pace. A Blake man in the cart stood up and fired a shot back towards the pursuers, which caused one of the following horses to shy, killing its rider. To this day it is said that that part of what was then the main Waterford–Kilkenny road, near Danesfort Cross, is haunted. The robbers took refuge in the avenue leading to the Wemys family home, Danesfort House, before dumping the statue in brambles near what is now Walsh's field.

Some say that it was the son of the Wemys who was involved in the infamous Hell Fire Club in Dublin, who erected the statue near the turret, facing towards Scotland, from where the Wemys family was thought to have originated before coming to Kilkenny, and where the last Wemys male heir went having gone broke. The statue was known around Danesfort as 'The Scotchman'. It was eventually bought from Mr Walsh by the famous

Grattan-Bellew family of Mount Loftus, between Gowran, Skeoughvosteen and Goresbridge, in 1939.

There was supposed to be a curse on the statue. Not only was a man killed during the pursuit of the robbers, but when the statue was removed from Walsh's field, the three men who moved it for the Grattan-Bellews all died in traffic accidents within a year. Tutankhamun eat your heart out!

We learn from Frank McEvoy that in the 1920s some likely lads from Danesfort sawed off one of the arms of the statue and attempted to sell it in Kilkenny city to the late Johnny Flood, who recognised it. The lads ran from his shop, taking the arm with them, and threw it in a pond in Danesfort. It is said that when the pond was drained it was found and used by a local farmer to tie down cocks of hay and that it was eventually lost. We know that in 1957 the statue missing the right arm was sold to John Hunt of Bailey, Howth, in Dublin. On his death in 1981, his widow, Mrs Gertrude Hunt, disposed of it. And there the trail of the Metal Man, the Scotchman, goes cold. Was he sold for scrap or will he turn up?

When I first delved into the history of the turret, the Wemys clan and Danesfort House, thanks to the promptings of an archaeologist, the words of this poem I learned in primary school came back to me:

Cad a dhéanfaimid feasta gan adhmad?
Tá deireadh na gcoillte ar lár;

níl trácht ar Chill Cháis ná a teaghlach
is ní bainfear a cling go bráth.

(Now what will we do for timber,
With the last of the woods laid low?
There's no talk of Cill Chais or its household
And its bell will be struck no more.)[4]

All that is left of Danesfort House, built in the middle of the seventeenth century, is the front portico, which was bought by the late Terence Hutchinson in the 1890s and is now attached to the front of Kellsboro House, Kells. The house was important because without it the turret would never have been built. A cattle dealer from Kerry, Con O'Sullivan, bought Danesfort House when the Wemys family fortune ran dry in the mid-1800s and he sold the stones from the house to the county council for two shillings a box. In fact, he stayed with the Irelands of Ballyda while he was buying the house.

Frank McEvoy's interviews with the late Joseph Ireland, Ballyda (1909–96), the father of current Fine Gael councillor for the area, Billy Ireland, and the late Mrs Ann Doyle (née Hayes) provided some fascinating history of the old house. Joseph Ireland told him that even as far back as the turn of the twentieth century, there was a swimming pool at Danesfort House, while Mrs Doyle,

---

4   This translation is by Thomas Kinsella.

who was born in 1890, recalled sliding down the banisters of the deserted house and stated that the waxed floors stood out in her memory.

The National Roads Authority (NRA) carried out archaeological investigations close to Danesfort Turret before building the motorway close by, over the site of an old road. It was discovered that one of the Wemys family had a cottage built on the side of the old road. The Wemys had built their palatial home near the road for trade purposes and the cottage was actually a bakery where travellers would buy food and drink, like an early version of a MacDonald's drive-thru, and this was just one facet of their business empire. They had also been given control of fairs in Bennettsbridge and other villages, held a number of times a year by the Butlers of Ormonde, and these brought much-wanted revenue to the fun-loving Wemys clan.

The placing of the turret was no accident. We learn from archaeologist Cóilín Ó Drisceoil that the ring fort dating back to pre-Christian times on the site was later inhabited by the early Anglo-Norman invaders around the thirteenth century, when the defence system was upgraded. It is safe to assume that this oval platform was protected by a bank and then a ditch, wherein there would have been military and residential buildings. From here you could see your enemies coming from a long way off, which made it easier to defend. And so when the whimsical Wemys family decided to build a hunting den, it was the logical location. Even today, from the bottom of the turret there are fine 360-degree views of the local landscape, and just to sit on the wall of the turret and take in the surroundings is wonderful. It's amazing that the hill on which it sits, with such an important role in the life of the community, has never been named.

Grannagh Castle

Sailing, tide assisted, up the River Suir, after crossing a sea, Irish or Atlantic, masters of their crafts had a clear passage until they reached Grannagh, where a large, imposing castle right on the bank came into view and stopped them in their tracks. And because the deepest channel was close to the fortress, they had to steer a course towards it and pay the tax for travelling upriver to Carrick-on-Suir, Portlaw, Cahir and Clonmel. French, Italian (mainly wool traders), Flemish and English vessels paid their dues, knowing that if they did not they would not get upriver, or, if they managed to avoid the castle, they certainly wouldn't get back down. Today, standing precariously on the outside wall, you can still see how close to it the boats and ships going up and down the River Suir, to Carrick-on-Suir and beyond, must have had to pass.

Grannagh Castle (from the Irish meaning gravelly place) played a huge part in the rich history of Kilkenny, Waterford and the south-east. It started life as a dun or fort owned by a local chieftain, Brawn,[5] presumably as a

---

5   Brawn appears to have been of Welsh extraction.

base from which to repel incursions by Norsemen from the settlement in Waterford city. However, it was not until the arrival of the Countess of Granny, Margaret Butler, in the middle of the sixteenth century, that Grannagh Castle became a symbol of power on the Irish political scene. Previous to this it was the subject of a bitter, all-consuming rivalry between the Norman purebreds, the de la Poers (Powers) and the more politically canny Butlers of Ormonde, also of Norman extraction. The Powers initially held all of Waterford and the area around Grannagh, County Kilkenny, including the river crossing there. They actually built the stone fortification at Grannagh in the late fourteenth century, but after they went to war against the nobles of Waterford city, against the wishes of the king, their fate was sealed and they were outlawed. The Butlers, who nearly always managed to choose the winning side in any conflict, supported the monarchy and were granted the castle.

James Butler, the 3rd Earl of Ormonde, took possession of the castle and the thousands of acres that came with it. The castle became the first line of defence against subsequent Power attempts to regain control of it and the accompanying lands. It comprised a large, square, walled enclosure with cylindrical corner towers. The landward side was later rebuilt by the Butlers, but the old river façade (late thirteenth century) survives, complete with its south-west tower, parts of the north-east tower and the connecting wall. In the late fourteenth century, the Butlers built a tall tower house in the north corner of the old castle and this was later extended by the addition of a two-storey dining hall. The oriel window, high up in the tower, was added in the seventeenth century. The surviving walls have some remnants of sculpted ornamentation, including an angel holding the Butler arms which decorates the inside arch of the window from which the Countess Margaret hung rebels. There is also a fine carving of St Michael the Archangel with the scales of justice.

In 1837 Samuel Lewis recorded in *A Topographical Dictionary of Ireland* that 'Granny or Grandison Castle, in Iverk, is one of the most considerable: it was the residence of Margaret Fitzgerald, the great Countess of Ormond, a lady of uncommon talents and qualifications, who is said also to have built the castles of Balleen and Coolkill, with several others of minor note.'

This makes the neglect of Grannagh Castle by official-dom today all the harder to understand. It is in complete contrast to the position of authority it held in the golden period of the Butler dynasty.

Piers Roe (Rua) Butler was the 8th Earl of Ormonde. On 6 March 1522, the king appointed him Lord Deputy of Ireland, an office he held until 13 May 1524 when he became Lord Treasurer. In his lifetime he amassed vast tracts of land and important concessions from the kings of England. Around 1485, he married Lady Margaret, daughter of Gerald Fitzmaurice Fitzgerald, 8th Earl of Kildare. Margaret didn't lack ambition, or the courage to act on it, actively controlling and increasing her land holdings when possible. She and her husband were responsible for the 'Camelot' years at Grannagh, spending much of their time there. The marriage was political, and they schemed and murdered their way to the highest office and influence. Grannagh became the main Butler castle, putting others like Kilkenny in the shade.

One story about the countess has been retold for generations: one day she summoned her jester to Grannagh and ordered him to lift her gloomy mood. He failed to make her laugh and, as a last resort, the court clown suggested a rope trick. He quickly fashioned a rope with several nooses. She responded by demanding to see the invention work. The countess ordered her soldiers to round up several peasants and warned the jester that if the invention was not successful, he would hang. Seven innocent people were hung from the battlements, an atrocity which apparently restored the countess' good spirits. It is said that she was so delighted with 'the Butler Knot' that she had it incorporated into the family coat of arms!

While it doesn't feature greatly in The Ormonde Deeds, the largest single collection of medieval deeds and records now extant in Ireland, Grannagh Castle had a certain prestige that others failed to match. It was a major military installation, held sway over a vast area and boasted the first ferry across the River Suir, presumably where Grannagh Boat Club is now located. In the north-east corner stood the main 'keep' or what was the most heavily fortified section of the castle. It was four storeys high and, as always, the most important people lived at the top. It stood nobly against the tidal Suir and projected an air of authority: the authority of the countess and her husband, which few dared to question. The now grass-covered courtyard led to the large dining hall, which was once the centre of activity, and great feasts were held there at certain times of the year. It is still surrounded by thick walls with once proud battlements, the remnants of which can still be seen today.

However, the castle is in a bad state at present, a shadow of its former self. Its ramparts were robbed over the centuries, the materials being used in the building of many local cottages. When the motorway and new bridge over the Suir were built nearby it was thought that Grannagh would receive a boost, but this has not proved to be the case. The area around it now has two huge overflow pipes connected inside a green metal railing that feeds into what was an old stream that flowed into the Suir under a lovely old stone arched bridge.

Today there are issues with access because the piece of ground between the castle and the road is in private ownership and there is a problem with insurance for the landowner. On the other hand, there is a right of way and it is a public monument under the care of the Office of Public Works (OPW). However, there has been no major political will over the last thirty years to showcase the beauty, elegance and importance – historically, socially and aesthetically – of Grannagh Castle.

In the last year the locals have rotavated and reseeded the area, cleared the pathways around the castle of weeds, carried out planting of the embankment and repaired and painted the picnic tables. Kilkenny County Council has cleared away overgrowth. The council has also repaired a section of the wall and of the pathway where there was some deterioration in the surface quality. Hopefully this will inspire more work on a worthy Irish antiquity.

Knockroe Passage Tomb

The Druid's Altar, the Newgrange of the south-east, the Red Hill, the Coshel; whatever you call it, Knockroe Passage Tomb is by far the most important, intricate, complex and mysterious prehistoric site in the Kilkenny region and its secrets are still literally being unearthed. It predates the Pyramids of Egypt and is considerably older than Newgrange or Stonehenge. To this day it is used for pagan worship and all sorts of people go there to get closer to nature. Modern-day druids and others visit, cognisant of what Knockroe is – a special place where ancient clans came to bury their dead, to celebrate the coming of the new year and to give thanks to the gods out of respect and fear of the elements. It is part of a series of similar sites dotted around the local landscape.

For a stranger, it can be a hard place to find. There is no signpost telling you where it is. To get there you drive to Callan from Kilkenny city and take the road to Carrick-on-Suir. At the slate quarries and opposite the fantastic pub, John Delaney's, you turn right and at the top of the hill, with the slate quarries on your right, you turn right (not left as I did) and go on a couple of hundred yards before turning right again and passing through a farmyard.

The monument, known locally as 'The Caiseal', has two passages on the southern side. The eastern passage has a cruciform chamber with a sill stone towards the front, with very large kerbstones on the southern side arcing around to the western passage. Quartz is scattered around the site. Although the western passage has a simpler design, it is the more interesting of the two, as it is aligned to allow the light of the winter solstice to penetrate the passage, and on both sides of the entrance are several large graded orthostats (large rocks) that give the impression of a court when viewed from the front.

Knockroe resonates with the people who have used it over the centuries: it is a place where cremations were held and sacrifices made; where depictions of life at the time of its construction were chiselled onto the huge boulders used to link the two chambers which are still evident today. It draws people like a magnet, and when they leave they feel enhanced by the experience of just having been there. Every 21 December, the shortest day of the year, people come to the Liguan Valley, called after the river of the same name that separates Kilkenny from Tipperary, to watch the sun set in precise alignment with the length of the west tomb. Knockroe was built as part of ancient sun-worship practices and it is one of a group of burial mounds which are geographically aligned in the landscape with the large mound on the summit of Slievenamon.

When discussing this tomb, it is important to mention Professor Muiris O'Sullivan of University College Dublin, because he has shed so much light on what went on in these monuments in pre-Christian times. He has made Knockroe his *magnum opus*, and if it had not been for his research and hard work, Knockroe would not be in the wonderful state of preservation that it is in today. When I first visited the site, twenty-three years ago, black polythene sheeting was strewn around it, access was very difficult and it was deteriorating even more quickly than it had in all the millennia before. Now the site has been excavated, restored to its original plan, preserved, cleaned up in the proper manner and fenced off. It is hugely impressive and it has the wow factor.

Professor O'Sullivan discovered in 2010 that on 21 December the sun shines into the outer compartment of the west tomb at Knockroe, but that the light veers off the straight line of the setting sun and faces slightly further north than the setting point of the sun. He explained that it seems as if the entrance arrangement was deliberately changed in ancient times, possibly relating to an expansion or restructuring of the overall complex, and further work will have to be carried out to elaborate on that assessment.

I went there on the longest day of the year and there was no sun, but that didn't matter because the alignment of the west tomb doesn't allow the sun to come into the chamber on 21 June.

According to Professor O'Sullivan, the tomb at

Knockroe has provided a treasure trove of information about the Neolithic Age and it has a gallery of weather-beaten, eroded megalithic art. Some of the artwork in the west tomb is very similar to decoration at the famous site on the island of Gavrinis, Brittany, and several of the decorated stones show a marked similarity between Knockroe and Newgrange in the Boyne Valley.

Nobody, however, had a better feeling for Knockroe than Sean Power, who was born a few yards from it in a cottage that is now derelict. The widower had an honesty that is rare and a knowledge of Knockroe that no expert could match. He died in 2012, the last person to be born at Knockroe. He witnessed the white witches and others coming down from Kilkenny and other parts on the shortest day of the year to pay homage to deities or spirits. They performed what could easily be described as mumbo jumbo, but Sean understood their need to let loose and their appreciation of this place, and he never judged them. He smiled at the thought of them and threw back his head as if to say they couldn't help it. He also told me that he had heard the stories of late-night/early-morning witches' covens using the place, but he never saw them. Sean understood why they came to Knockroe, for the same reason he never left – he felt he belonged there. Growing up there he never witnessed anything out of the ordinary, but explained that for him and for others it is a sacred spot and holds a special place in the hearts of the older people in the locality.

It is well worth visiting the tomb to see just how inventive our ancestors were and how these tombs were not built on a whim, but as part of a series of aligned cairns that have survived. Knockroe is a magical place, from the tomb itself with its aligned chambers and quartz rock, to the beauty of the surrounding area with the River Liguan 150 yards away, and Coonan's Hill and Carraigdoon facing you.

Close by is Kilmacoliver Hill, on the summit of which is a 4,000-year-old ring of boulders. Most are equidistant from each other; there are just three exceptions – two large stones on the west side are closer to each other, forming a V-shape and almost touching, while there is one single boulder on the east side which stands somewhat apart from its neighbouring stones. Sadly this individual stone is no longer upright. Pat Nolan of the Kilkenny Archaeological Society has described how amazing it is, standing behind the fallen boulder at Kilmacoliver, to watch the sun slowly descend into the groove between the two western stones, until it becomes a single prick of light and then disappears.

Although Knockroe is noted in research carried out for the Ordnance Survey in the nineteenth century by Slieverue man John O'Donovan, it was not until the 1980s and the work of local antiquarian Johnny Maher and Con Manning from the National Monument Service that Knockroe was, so to speak, put on the map. And without Professor Muiris O'Sullivan, there is no telling what would have happened to Knockroe. We owe him and his team from University College Dublin a huge debt for what they have done and continue to do.

The OPW has sometimes been criticised for not giving enough care to various hidden heritage gems in County Kilkenny, but here at Knockroe it is doing a fantastic job in a complex situation to enhance our knowledge. The plan is eventually to have the site opened up to as large a volume of people as possible, without affecting its integrity.

Kilcreene Lodge

V ery few homes in Ireland have as rich a history as Kilcreene Lodge, once the Smithwick family home. A short distance from the centre of the city, it sits on twenty-three acres with its own lake, woods and the River Breagagh, a tributary of the River Nore, flowing close by. It boasts a waterfall, all sorts of wildlife and has strong links to famous people from the past, including The Liberator, Daniel O'Connell, who stayed there many times and was a great friend of the family. This wonderful private property was also a retreat for the rich and famous, such as US film stars with strong Irish connections. Here, too, the Irish aristocracy came to be wined and dined by the Smithwick family, who had power and influence far beyond the city walls. Lord Iveagh and his wife Miranda (of the Guinness family) were regulars.

It is easy to see why no one ever turned down an invitation to visit what is a most beautiful place. Kilcreene Lodge is timeless and to walk into it is like walking into another world. It is hard to believe that you are so close to the hustle and bustle of city life. The main entrance used to be down by the Butts, from a small road adjacent to the Waterbarracks, which now leads to black metal gates that are permanently closed. The present owners, Gerry and Christine Byrne, use the entrance opposite Daly's Hill on the Ballycallan Road, just after Kennyswell Bridge. Christine and Gerry, who own the Left Bank, Hibernian Hotel and Blue Bar in Kilkenny, have done a marvellous job on the house and grounds, and we owe them a huge debt for keeping such a priceless hidden gem intact and in such excellent condition.

But to understand Kilcreene Lodge's significance we must go back to Kilcreene House, which was knocked down many years ago and was located where Kilcreene Hospital now stands. It was originally owned by the Rothes and came into the possession of the Smithwicks when they purchased the brewery and lands around St Francis's Abbey in the 1800s. However, the Smithwicks never occupied the house, which was demolished. Instead they lived in Kilcreene Lodge, which was built around 1690 and redeveloped a number of times. John Smithwick, the son of Edmond Smithwick (d. 1876) was the first of the family to live at Kilcreene Lodge (from 1861) after his marriage to Christina Devereux, whose father owned a distillery in Bishopswater in County Wexford. They spent considerable money on the lodge and grounds, and it quadrupled in size during their lives. A very fine chandelier was purchased from Baccarat, France, and installed in an extension to the lodge built in 1884. This coincided with a huge increase in activity at the Smithwick's Brewery and it is sad that after over 300 years in operation it will close by the end of 2013. Many feel that if the Smithwick family still had it, the brewery would still be in business.

The last member of the family to run the brewery, up to the 1960s, was Walter Smithwick, a much-loved man who was famous for translating the ancient book of Kilkenny, the *Liber Primus Kilkenniensis*, from Latin to English. He was a solicitor by profession and his soirées and garden parties at Kilcreene were highlights of the year to which everyone seemed to be invited. He loved Kilcreene and loved to share it with his family and friends, and the last great party held there was to celebrate Walter's eightieth birthday around twenty-four years ago. His son, Paul, who inherited the house, felt the same way, but being a Dublin-based solicitor, he sold the lodge some time around 1990, because Kilcreene was just too big for him.

Kilcreene Lodge was originally a miller's house, and a retting pond used in the milling process can still be seen in the grounds. Retting involved moistening or soaking the flax to soften and separate the fibres by partially rotting it before carrying on the milling process.

The lake at Kilcreene was originally a millstream that was put in around 1871, with water diverted from the Breagagh. Water from the lake was used in the house. Walter Smithwick, in a talk to Kilkenny Archaeological Society in the 1960s, said it was the first house in County Kilkenny to have a bathroom with running water.

Many anglers in the Butts area of the city loved the fact that the lake was always stocked with fish because when the Breagagh flooded, so too would the lake, the sluice gates of which were then opened to release loads of fish down into the Breagagh; or so local historian and former *Kilkenny People* employee Seán Kerwick told me.

Everyone has a favourite memory of Kilcreene, Walter Smithwick and his charming wife Molly. Jimmy and Johnny Rhatigan, both retired from the brewery, were mesmerised when, as small boys, they saw Walter walk down the steps of the Club House Hotel with Tyrone Power, who was the Brad Pitt of his day and the star of many westerns and adventure films.

Paul Smithwick, the last member of the family to live at Kilcreene, speaks of an idyllic childhood full of wonderful people. He tells a story about Jimmy Cagney dancing on the parquet floor of the drawing room. An icon of American film, Cagney was the most important actor of his generation and a friend of the family.

Kilcreene is in safe hands. Thanks to the Byrnes we still have a priceless gem in our midst.

Tory Hill

M ade famous in the eighteenth and nineteenth centuries by notorious rapparees (highway men) with lingering rumours of hidden treasure and secret chambers, Tory Hill has a special place in the hearts of the people of South Kilkenny. The word Tory derives from the Irish *tóraidhe*, meaning outlaw, or more precisely, one who is being pursued. An older name for the hill is said to be *Sliabh gCruinn*, meaning mountain of trees, although Canon Carrigan does not accept this in his book on the history of the diocese of Ossory written around 1900. According to the Canon, Tory Hill was the finishing point of the Barony of Ida and he claims that the name does not mean mountain of trees but the mountain of the tribe of Uí Crinn.

Set 966 feet above sea level (only forty-four feet short of mountain status), the hill offers commanding views of the rich countryside on all sides and you can see Tramore beach on a clear day as well as an outline of Duncannon and the new bridge linking Kilkenny and Waterford, which looks like a large water spray from fifteen miles away. And on a Wednesday morning in April, in the company of photographer Charlie Maher, I gazed at the ferry leaving Rosslare for Fishguard in Wales from the Marian Cross at the top of Tory Hill. The hilltop has seen continuous use as a refuge for thousands of years, going back to 4,000 BC when, allegedly, the Greeks were there.

Tory Hill is the recent name given to the site and it memorialises two highwaymen associated with the hill – Edward and James Denn. However, it is its association with Freney the Robber, a highwayman of the latter part of the 1700s, that is still best remembered in the area. Freney, who supposedly took from the rich and gave to the poor, used the hill to escape from his English pursuers in much the same way as Edward Denn did before him. The hill is full of hollows and, with its covering of trees and undergrowth, would have been perfect for hiding from pursuing soldiers. Local folklore also says there is a cave on the hill that could be used to conceal a horse and rider.

While nothing is recorded about the life of James Denn, a little is known of Edward. He was very popular with the local people, who, despite offers of gold and other inducements, refused to give any information on him to the authorities. Local historian Seán Maher told me Denn is buried in Dunkitt Graveyard in Kilmacow.

Freney on the other hand was a much more flamboyant character: an Irish Robin Hood. His name was uttered with a mixture of fear and awe, and he was one of the few highwaymen to escape the hangman's noose. In his forties Freney gave up the highway and turned respectable, becoming a customs and excise officer at New Ross Port, which can be seen from the top of Tory. He later went on to write his memoirs and these are housed in Kilkenny County Library. However, he snitched on the rest of his gang to save his own skin and they were all hanged. Michael Holden from Kilfane, Thomastown, has written an excellent biography of Freney, which is well worth a read.

With a number of ancient sites on its slopes, including the Farnogue Court Tomb, Tory Hill is a hidden gem and, though overshadowed by Brandon Hill in some respects, has a fascinating history. While it has been used as a shelter for those avoiding the law, it is the long history of pagan pageantry and idolatry on Tory Hill that sets it apart from religious sites such as Brandon Hill.

Although a Christian cross has now been erected on its summit, it is to the druids that we must turn when considering the historical significance of this place. Because of its location, it was a natural spot for burials and a front altar at the Farnogue Tomb that dates back thousands of years before Christianity makes it clear that these holy men were central in glorifying deities at this spot. Located on the eastern slope of Tory Hill, overlooking a visually stunning valley with a small tributary of the Munster Blackwater, the Farnogue Court Tomb is the only one in the county and one of the most southerly in Ireland. The tomb is orientated NE–SW and consists of three chambers, one erect stone at the façade and some kerbstones around the edge of the sub-trapezoidal cairn. The south chamber measures twenty-three feet in length, the central chamber is ten feet in length and the north chamber thirteen feet long. The chambers are separated by sill stones and are three feet below the present ground level. No roof stones remain and the court was later incorporated into a field boundary. A very substantial amount of the cairn remains in place and drops off steeply to the east.

On the second Sunday of July every year the hill welcomes hundreds of people for Fraughan or Fraochan Sunday. The rosary is recited and a hymn sung at the Marian Cross erected in 1954, but this is only a very recent initiative. For thousands of years the people of the area came to Tory to celebrate the summer festival of Lughnasa and to eat the wild berries, which, it has been claimed, intoxicated them as they fermented in their stomachs. There is a long history of gathering and eating these fraochans (a form of blueberry from the vaccinium family) and a number of studies have shown they have healing properties and are excellent antioxidants. This knowledge has been passed down through the generations and a few older people still pick and eat them. According to folklore, the berries, which do not ripen fully until the middle of July, were traditionally used to cure diarrhoea, dysentery, haemorrhoids, gastrointestinal inflammation, scurvy and urinary complaints. Decoctions of the leaves, we are told, were also used internally for diabetes and externally for inflammation of the eyes and mouth, infections and burns.

And of course there is the mystery of an inscription found on a large stone somewhere on the hill. In his book, *The Statistical Observations relative to the County Kilkenny*, William Tighe claimed that the words 'Beli Diuose' on the stone came from the Pelasgian era, referring to the indigenous inhabitants of the Aegean Sea region and their cultures before the advent of the Greek language. However, we learn from Seamus Davis of Tullaroan that the authenticity of the inscription was questioned in the 1840s and the stone was examined around 1850 at the Tighe residence in Woodstock, where it had been carefully preserved. Rev. James Greaves, archaeologist of the Kilkenny Archaeological Society, accompanied by the secretary, conducted the investigation. They found the inscription to be modern and crudely carved, with some letters differing significantly to those in Tighe's drawing. Greaves said it required too many leaps of faith and stretches of the imagination to read it as 'Beli Diuose', but amazingly, when a sketch of it was reversed it read unmistakably as E CONIC 1731. Their assessment was corroborated by a letter from Dr John O'Donovan from Slieverue, topographer, historian and the greatest Irish scholar of his time. O'Donovan, whose grandfather knew Edmond (Ned) Conic well, explained that Ned, a millstone cutter, had carved his name and the date on the stone one morning while waiting for his fellow workers, who had remained drinking in Mullinavat. Having lain flat on the hill for several years, the stone was raised on supports and turned upside down by youths who were making a fence for a jumping contest. The inscription was then discovered by one of the Tighes.

Unless you have a good pair of walking shoes don't go to Tory Hill, as there is no vehicular access. You will have to wash your shoes in the little bath at the barrier because of the incidence of tree disease and the risk of spreading it. At the time of writing, the barrier to the top of the hill has had to be locked because of the huge increase in illegal tree felling and robbery at the state-owned forestry. As soon as Coillte workers put up a new barrier and locks, they are cut and removed. We hope that soon the gardaí will apprehend these criminals and the entrance can once again be left unlocked. There is no better way to spend an afternoon than on Tory Hill.[6]

---

6   Trail Kilkenny has two different walks depending on how much time you have and how fit you feel. They can be obtained on www.trailkilkenny.ie

Rothe House

❦

Every inch of Rothe House drips with history. It is a complex of three Tudor houses and three courtyards behind which are a garden, orchard and vegetable garden, along with a well. They are all inter-connected and the size of the complex increased steadily in size as the fortunes of the merchant family that owned it, the Rothes, improved. The three houses are built one behind the other, the first completed in 1594, the second in 1604 and the third in 1610. Named after the merchant prince John Rothe Fitz Piers, who shipped silks and fine clothes to Kilkenny from Bristol and northern France, it is the only uncontaminated Tudor building in the city centre and started life as a family home and shop, selling the silks and other fabrics Rothe imported.

A mere seventeen footsteps and you have passed it, the beautifully limestone-clad building on the city's Parliament Street which holds the key to the most successful period in Kilkenny's history – the golden era from which so much invaluable information and objects have been saved. Rothe House was part of what was called 'Ye Faire City' when the Irish Catholic Confederation, or Confederation of Kilkenny, ruled Ireland, and when the city, and not Dublin, was considered the capital of the country. From 1642 onwards, after a popular uprising, the majority of the country was controlled by the Confederate Catholics and they received papal blessing with the arrival of Cardinal Rinuccini to the centre of administration of the confederation in Kilkenny, which was destroyed when Cromwell invaded Ireland in 1649.

Rothe House was used as a school from the late eighteenth century well into the nineteenth century and the great John Banim, the nineteenth-century Kilkenny author, went to school here. In one of his novels he gives a wonderful description of this time:

> Jammed in between two mere modern houses with shop windows, there was in it a curious old structure, or rather a succession of curious old structures, situated to the rear of this introductory one. Here Father O'Connell put his adopted son to school ... All the nooks and corners of the odd, old place, were all, all the playgrounds of him and his fellow school-fellows. He will stop to this day, before the streetward archway, and look into the two quadrangles, until recollected pleasure becomes present pain ... What hour of satiated passion, what hour of worldly success, has been worth one minute of the passionless, thoughtless pleasures, experienced within the intricacies and the quaintnesses of the odd, old place?

In 1962 the house was bought by Kilkenny Archaeological Society with John Brennan, who already had a butcher's shop in the front house and was a very popular figure in the city. In 1966 the Kilkenny Archaeological Society opened the doors of their museum, and later what had been Brennan's butchers on the other side of the gated entrance was added to this. It was purchased from Timothy O'Hanrahan, who had already spent a fortune restoring the house. Shortly, the iconic gated entrance to the first and second courtyards of Rothe House will be open to all, as the shop that is now housed in this part of the building moves from the front of the complex to the third house.

It is the open space of the second courtyard that really allows you to breathe in the Tudor element of Rothe House – where you half expect to hear *Hamlet*'s Polonius giving advice to Laertes, or Portia delivering the famous 'quality of mercy' speech from *The Merchant of Venice*. However, there is continuity to the Ireland of both the past and present on this site. In the second courtyard is a cist grave dating from the Bronze Age, around 4,000 years ago, and a food vessel that was buried under it forms part of the intriguing archaeological display in the third house. In the late 1890s the Gaelic League in Kilkenny was founded here by Timothy O'Neill and the same room is still used for the governing body of the society's monthly meetings. Thomas MacDonagh, a signatory of the 1916 Proclamation, taught here in 1903, while Peter DeLoughry, who made the key which opened the lock to free Éamon de Valera from Lincoln Jail in England in 1919, had his foundry at the rear of Rothe House.

The Phelan and Lanigan rooms are more or less the same as they were back when the first house was built in 1594. In the Lanigan room there is an incredible truss roof made without any metal screws or nails. But the Phelan room in particular is a wonderful example of Tudor architecture. Antlers dating back 10,000 years from a Great Irish Deer (long extinct) are set high on the wall in this room above the limestone fireplace dating from the construction of the house. They were found close to Swift's Heath, just outside the city, where Dean Jonathan Swift spent his childhood. The walls of the room are lined with portraits of the Irish painter Sir John Lavery and his wife, the ravishing Lady Hazel, which the family donated to Rothe House.

Within the walls of the three houses are also conserved irreplaceable pieces of Kilkenny history that have been bequeathed or gifted to Kilkenny Archaeological Society by families who know the society will look after them, cherish them and put them on public display or make them available to researchers.

Donations from the city, county and all over the world are displayed in the house. Each room has been given its own story from Kilkenny's past. For example, in one room the story of Godwin Meade Swifte, 2nd Viscount Carlingford and an eccentric relation of Dean Jonathan Swift, is commemorated. In 1857 he designed and constructed a 'plane' at Swift's Heath. The propeller and wooden wheel of the ill-fated contraption hang on the wall.

Its one and only voyage was from the top of Foulksrath Castle, and Swift's Heath had to be altered to allow its removal from the main dining room, where construction was carried out, because the viscount hadn't measured the entrance properly. Other items of interest include a Viking sword donated by a Mrs Kinivan, numerous rare books and manuscripts in the library, and the Toler-Aylward collection, the largest costume collection in the country, from which a small number of dresses are on display, including the trousseau of Lady Eleanor Butler who married Hector Charles Toler-Aylward of Shankill Castle in 1894. It is intended to include a large selection from the Toler-Aylward costumes in a new exhibition currently being designed, which will be presented as part of the Renaissance project: the final piece of the jigsaw in the rejuvenation of Rothe House.

As far as we know the last person born in the house was the artist Carmel Delaney-Mooney, and a photograph of her in her pram outside Rothe House can be seen on the wall. The Power family are well represented, with portraits and personal effects on display: a portrait of Sir John Power who gave us Kilfane Waterfall hangs in the Langton room, while an extraordinary painting of his brother, Sir John, who founded the Kilkenny Theatre, is on another wall as you go down the stairs from that room – he looks very comfortable in hosiery as Hamlet.

Remnants of the ten great merchant families of Kilkenny – Archdeken, Archer, Cowley, Langton, Lee,

Knaresborough, Lawless, Raggett, Rothe and Shee – are also found here. Many of the stone plaques that would have been set in the front walls of their homes, now vanished, are in the second courtyard, while others are in the grounds of St Mary's Church. However, the Rothe's plaque with the family crest is still embedded in the front wall on Parliament Street.

The garden attached to the house boasts a corbelled well used by monks in the twelfth century and the first section includes a vegetable and herb garden laid out as it would have been when Rothe was in situ. It is an oasis of calm in the centre of the city and it seems likely that Cardinal Rinuccini would have walked here during the Confederation of Kilkenny. This garden provides the modern visitor with a glimpse into what life would have been like for the occupants back in the late sixteenth and early seventeenth centuries.

As you would expect with such an old site, there are claims of spirits, ghosts and unusual happenings, inexplicable in normal terms. But these are of a good type according to Róisín McQuillan, one of the staff, who tries to deflect any questions of that nature.

Margaret M. Phelan explained the importance of Rothe House to me:

> In Ireland we know much more about the priest in his medieval monastery, the lord in his feudal castle, than we do about the important trader, his family and workers. We

have many more churches and castles than we have merchant homes. So it is impossible to overrate the great importance of Rothe House, its service to the present community, and its dignified, gracious reflection of times gone past.

Here, too, is housed a library without equal in terms of Kilkenny's heritage. To walk into the library at Rothe House is one of the great pleasures of life and, under the stewardship of librarian Edward Law, this place is in safe hands. Every book ever written about Kilkenny is here, along with all the graveyard inscriptions from around the county. Kilkenny's great literary figures are not forgotten and the works of the Banim brothers, Francis MacManus and Francis Hackett, Earl of Desart, are here. It also holds maps, including the Grand Jury maps of Kilkenny from the early 1800s which were discovered in a local solicitor's office. There is a superb holding of all local newspapers from the 1780s, including the *Kilkenny People*.

The most important book in the library is *The New Testament* printed at Rhemes by John Fogny in 1582. There is also a first edition of the Roman Catholic version of the New Testament in English, donated by an American descendant of a Kilkenny family. One of Francis Hackett's books, in a special binding, has this humorous presentation inscription to his sister: 'One of 25 copies I had bound specially. I am too delicate to number the 25. So you can choose a nice low number for yourself.' The archive includes a variety of material from the 1700s onwards: deeds, manuscripts, family papers, club and charity minutes, commercial records and a fascinating collection of business letterheads from the 1870s through to the 1960s.

Rothe House has offered a family-history research service to those of Kilkenny ancestry for many years. Recently this has been extended to a practical online facility available 24/7 to anyone wishing to trace their Irish origins. RootsIreland.ie has over twenty million records of baptisms, marriages and deaths augmented by some early census records (for example 1821), indexes to *Griffith's Valuation* and other sources proving invaluable to those either filling in a family tree or starting to seek their Irish roots. Backed up by a personal enquiry service, this has proved popular to the many users of the service. Locally one can always visit the member's library.

With its three separate houses, courtyards and huge garden, Rothe House is the foundation on which the Kilkenny Archaeological Society (KAS) has built a world-class collection of antiquities, historical gems, archaeological pieces and a seemingly limitless library on Kilkenny. No wonder it is treated with such reverence by the voluntary body that owns it.

Grennan Castle

I n 1655 Grennan Castle, Thomastown, was described by
an English commentator as a 'faire castle with many
outhouses, stables, large orchards, fishing ponds, and a
water mill for grinding corn' which, the writer said, was in
good repair. It boasted a courtyard wall inside which there
was probably a vegetable garden. It had its own forge and
bakery, and was self-sufficient, as well as being situated on
one of the best and most beautiful pieces of land in the
country. It was teeming with wildlife, it was a fantastic
fortification and was easily twice the size of the ordinary
keeps that later passed for castles. It also had a fosse, part
of the original earthworks of the motte and bailey built
by Thomas Fitz Anthony (c. 1210), on which the castle,
which was probably finished by his son-in-law after his
death, sits. Grennan, which translates as 'palace', was only
bested in the region by Kilkenny Castle and was much
sought-after over the centuries, with countless quarrels,
fights and legal disputes about who owned it.

Of course the River Nore gave it life and archaeologist
Ben Murtagh described the river, a hundred yards from the
castle, as a bit like the M50 of the Middle Ages, such was
the volume of traffic on it. Even now, it is almost hypnotic,

and from the top of the castle you can hear the river water on the bend more clearly than you can at ground level. It is like a natural theatre with everything echoing; even the clamour of the crows and the drudgery of the traffic on the Thomastown–Inistioge Road, which overlooks the castle on the far side of the river, reverberates, it seems, with increased volume.[7]

At the sub-ground floor level of the castle there was a wine cellar, and most of the wine stored there would have come up the River Nore by boat. Above this there are three arched chambers (barrel-vaulted with stone), which themselves comprised two storeys in medieval times. They have now been converted into barns with the walls knocked out to help the cattle to get in and out without difficulty. The arched ceilings are still in place, but are at risk of collapse without restoration. Directly above was the fifty-foot long stateroom and at the south-east corner of the room there appears to have been a chapel. The entrance was at the riverside and was several feet off the ground.

There were two more storeys above the stateroom

---

7   To find Grennan Castle, exit Kilkenny city and go onto the ring road, turning for Thomastown at the appropriate roundabout. After four miles you arrive at the charming village of Bennettsbridge, home of hydro-powered Mosse Pottery. Go over the bridge and on to Thomastown, six miles further on. Follow the one-way system and again cross over the Nore and follow the signs for Thomastown GAA Club. If you park at the bridge in the centre of Thomastown, you can walk from there to the castle by the bank of the river.

supported by corbels (pieces of masonry jutting out of a wall to carry extra weight). Thankfully, the stairway up to these still stands in the north-east corner. The summit of the castle, sixty-five feet off the ground, has views of Jerpoint, Boherduff, Carrickmourne (home to the legendary Dixie Doyle), back into the Salmon Pool and over the bridge to Thomastown itself, with the parish church dominating. You can also make out the ruins of Grennan Church from here.

One family is synonymous with Grennan Castle. The Denns, who gave themselves such titles as Fulk and Baron of Kayer, were a law unto themselves and the self-styled masters of Thomastown and surroundings. W. J. Pilsworth in his captivating book, *History of Thomastown and District*, written in the 1950s, puts flesh on a legend recalled here that has never been discredited. The story goes that King Richard II of England visited Thomastown twice in 1395 and 1399 and it is said that he was livid with the Denn man who occupied Grennan and the lands surrounding it for not paying him taxes. He swore that he would have his head on a platter. So he made his way by boat to tidal Inistioge from New Ross and from there set out on horse-back for Grennan. After a mile or so, we are told, the king and his men came upon the first of numerous casks of good French red wine that had been left along the side of the road, of which they partook. On arrival at Grennan, the king, a little inebriated we assume, was welcomed by the woman of the house, a good-looking wench, although there was no sign of Denn. After pleasantries and more drink, he was led to the top of the stateroom for a banquet. A cart with a covered platter was wheeled up the centre of the aisle and when the cover was lifted, there was the head of Denn covered in blood. At this point, King Richard is supposed to have said:

> As grace be mine
> I'm sorry for the good knight's wine,
> I'd give a dozen of my men,
> For thy one life, my outlaw Den [*sic*].

Denn jumped up from underneath the platter and of course he was pardoned. According to Pilsworth, the account is most probably true, and he notes that there had been a dispute over succession of the lands and castle at this time.

Thomas Denn, Lord of Grennan, kept 'Papish priests' in hiding at the castle in 1610–11. By 1638 the Denns were at the height of their power, owning thousands of acres and holding various positions of power, such as sheriff, all over the south-east, making them one of the most important families in the region. In *Healy's History and Antiquities of Kilkenny*, published in 1884, we learn that in 1641 Thomas Denn had 386 acres at Grennan and that his relations, the Archdeacons (McOdys) had 58 acres there. The Denns also had a share in 335 acres at Smithstown in Thomastown. Another Denn, removed by

Cromwell during his conquest of Ireland, was not happy to go to Clare with the rest of the family, so became a rapparee, using Tory Hill in Mullinavat as his secret hideaway. Interestingly the family of Freney the Robber also laid legal claim to Grennan at one stage. Members of the Denn family seemed to turn on each other every second generation or so, as happened when 'Fulk' Denn took on, and subsequently killed, his brothers William and Richard over lands they held belonging to the Ormondes.

Eventually, abandoned and unoccupied, Grennan Castle came crumbling down many centuries later. It is now in a sad state. Canon Carrigan, in his history of the Diocese of Ossory written around 1900, says, 'Down to about 1830 the castle was still surrounded by a strong and high courtyard wall together with a great many ruins and minor appendages. Vandalism then stepped in and played havoc, fast and free with the noble ruin.' His words are echoed by W. J. Pilsworth, who notes on the subject of the castle's decline since the eighteenth century: 'And so today it stands, shorn of its beauties, a monument to man's ignorance and avarice, and the castle which was once a fitting residence for the highest in the land now gives shelter to the beasts of the land.'

We learn from archaeologist Ben Murtagh that many of the most valuable stones in the castle were removed, including the window and door frames. Among these were Dundry stones, which would have originated near Bristol and were the most expensive building material of the time; they would have been imported up the Nore by boat. Today, there are a few examples of Dundry stone still in the area that most probably came from Grennan Castle.

Today, there is not even a plaque on this once proud place to let casual passers-by, walking from the centre of town, know of its important history. Time and man have not been kind to the place and although its walls are nine feet thick at the base, the damage inside is enormous. The inside is in near total collapse. It is sad to see what could be a monument to rival Kilkenny Castle in such a state and it should now be shown some tender, loving care.

Jenkinstown Castle

❦

It is intriguing that one of Ireland's leading songwriters now lives in the place where one of our greatest ever musical ambassadors, Thomas Moore, wrote his most famous ballad, 'The Last Rose of Summer'. Jenkinstown Castle played a huge role in the life of the city and county of Kilkenny, with powerful, influential people living there. The castle had it all – Spanish heiresses; an owner whose first fiancée was beheaded with Marie Antoinette; an eccentric who preferred the company of animals to humans; tales of ghosts and tragedies; the visit of Thomas Moore, the Elvis Presley of his time – but little of the original building is left save for the front entrance, now incorporated into the front gates of St Kieran's College in Kilkenny city.

There is something in the air at Jenkinstown; you can feel it as you drive past the immaculately maintained Conahy GAA Club pavilion and pitches, and the well-kept, proud farms on either side. The land is rich and fertile and, as you turn right up the lane to where the castle once stood (and where the newly built parish church opened in the mid-1980s), there are all sorts of peculiar and lovely pieces of memorabilia perched along the gateway and border of the farmhouse closest to the original site.

It is important to differentiate between Jenkinstown House and Castle. Today we can get a sense of the castle's size by looking at the entrance to St Kieran's College, as it was one of the three original gateways to Jenkinstown Castle and was taken down stone by stone and rebuilt at the front of the college in the 1940s. The castle stood from the 1600s and its size and status went up and down along with the fortunes of those who owned it. One of these stands out – the eccentric James Bryan, who went by his Irish name, Seamus Briain. He was a recluse, who famously advertised a reward of fifty guineas in *Finn's Leinster Journal* of April 1801 for any information leading to the discovery of oak, ash and elm trees cut down at Jenkinstown and at nearby Gragara. He was a great man for ghost stories and piseogs. He never married, although he lived to be eighty-eight, and paid local people if they gave him good information on the deer and other wild animals that he sought. To this day, the grounds of Jenkinstown Park are home to a small herd of deer kept within the walled paddock by the woods. It is said that James Bryan was mad, but he still managed to increase the lands at Jenkinstown and he left a good estate for his nephew George Bryan, the man who made, perhaps, the greatest impression at Jenkinstown.

George witnessed the massacre at the Tuileries Palace during the French Revolution and his first fiancée was beheaded along with Marie Antoinette on 16 October 1793. He later married her sister, Countess Maria Louise

Augustine of Nancy, France. His wife, we are told: 'Had a kindness of heart that spread happiness not only throughout her own immediate family but that respectable circle in which she moved.' It helped that she had a fortune. George also had a fortune because his mother, from Oporto in Portugal, was the only daughter of a vastly wealthy merchant there. It was estimated that he was the wealthiest commoner in Ireland and added 169 acres of land at nearby Ballyrafton to his estate for £3,042.

There was great pomp associated with Jenkinstown Castle, as documented in 1803 when an unnamed visitor wrote of the owner, Major George Bryan: 'The demesne which is richly wooded is proportionate to the possessions of the hospitable proprietor who is a constant resident upon the noble estate.' He continues: 'The castle's internal arrangements are remarkably elegant and sumptuous. The entrance hall is a noble appointment, the great saloons and libraries are chaste designs and cleverly executed.' How things change.

It is striking that in the early 1800s many famous thespians and artistes, including Thomas Moore, went on stage at the castle, as is well documented in the Kilkenny Private Theatre Company records. The playwright Brinsley Sheridan performed his comedy *The Rivals* here in 1801. The play was US President George Washington's favourite and introduced the word malapropism to the English language.

The property eventually passed to the family of the

2nd Baron Bellew of Barmeath, of Barmeath Castle, Louth. They moved to Jenkinstown Castle in 1880 and superimposed heavy battlements of cut stone for effect. The battlements later collapsed and killed several workmen. The last titled person to live in the castle was Lady Bellew, who moved out in 1935, first to Kilcreene and then to Butler House on Patrick Street, Kilkenny, with an annuity of £500 a year. She died in March 1973 aged eighty-eight and is buried in St Kieran's cemetery.

In his excellent article in the *Old Kilkenny Review*, J. Brennan comments that the Bryans, who lived at Jenkinstown from 1640 to 1880, are completely forgotten and that the Bellews, who lived there from 1880 to 1935, are remembered by only a small few. Both families also had legal problems. If you think family inheritance is difficult now, just look at the will of John Bryan (dated 1 December 1673). Bryan had six children by his first wife Jane Loftus, and five by his second wife (who survived her husband), Ursula Walsh. The will is a deathbed plea to his eldest son to provide for his stepmother, brothers and sister, and stepbrothers and stepsisters. James is requested to honour an earlier promise that he would make certain monetary bequests to his siblings, and allow his stepmother to enjoy those lands that were held by the father and upon the same terms. The will also reveals both John's resentment of his current landless status, having handed over the estate to his son, and some fear that his wishes may not be honoured. I quote him:

I charge and require that my said son James Bryan not to molest or hinder her [Ursula Bryan] in the enjoyment thereof during her life, nor trouble or prejudice her or her children in anything, having given him an estate and having released unto him the great powers I had to charge him, though I received nothing of his portion, and having given unto him and paid for him and in the worst of times spent in providing and recovering the estate far more than the value thereof, and he performing my will therein I forgive him of all things wherein he offended me and I pray God to bless him and all my children.

We know from J. Brennan that the Bryans came to Jenkinstown, formerly known as *Corclach* (which translates as stumps of trees) around 1640, when John Bryan (John of Kilkenny), married an heiress, Ann Stanes. The family stayed in Jenkinstown for 240 years.

Jenkinstown House, where Mr Jimmy MacCarthy now lives, was built for Sir Patrick Bellew (1798–1866), and shows us what the castle looked like in its heyday. Macroom-born MacCarthy has brought some of the splendour back to the house since he purchased it six or seven years ago. We should be on our bended knees to the slightly reclusive musical genius for taking on the restoration of the house. The man who gave us songs such as 'Ride On', 'No Frontiers' and 'Come Running Home Again Katie' has made his home here, and as day breaks at around 4.50 a.m. and the sun rises on the slightly Gothic building, you can see why he has chosen to live here with a glorious view of Kilkenny in front of him and the fabulous, fabled woods behind. Here, we are told, ghosts roam, especially the Green Lady, who has been seen by several people and was described in *Erin's Own* by a now deceased soldier stationed there during the Emergency (1939–45).

Jimmy has also created, from the old church used by Catholics, then Protestants and then Catholics again, a wonderful soundproofed 106-seat theatre and recording studio. It is called, appropriately, the Thomas Moore Theatre. He has married the old with the new in a seamless way that has left the history of the place intact and provided it with a future – the theatre and recording studio.

Jenkinstown is well worth a visit and while the castle is gone, many little reminders remain, especially as you walk around.

Freestone Hill

⌒⬦⬦⌒

The fire lit up the night sky for miles around. Incantations rang out as the druids said their words of homage to the gods. And as the flames went higher, the community closed in to pay their last respects to their loved ones, sending them on their way, skywards. This is an imagined representation of a scene on Freestone Hill, situated on the southern ridge of the Castlecomer Plateau, from the third century, a hundred years before St Patrick came to Ireland.

The hill catches the eye as you drive from Kilkenny city to Carlow on the old road. You come to the Fox and Goose public house and as you reach the brow of the hill there, it meets you. You are faced by a lone, wind-shaped hawthorn tree perched on top of a hill. As you come closer, you can just make out the circle of a ring fort below the summit, and as you pass by Clara GAA Club you are struck by how it dominates its surroundings.

It doesn't have the same immediate appeal as Kilkenny Castle or some other sites in the county, but it is just as important in terms of our past and also how pre-Christian people lived in Ireland. There is a reverence attached to Freestone Hill that is not found everywhere. And a rural community watches over it and identifies itself by it – it is their logo if you like.

It has captivated ordinary people and experts alike, and the debate continues about the many Roman items found at Freestone Hill and the status of the sixteen people buried there, all burned beforehand, save one – a child. Many questions arise but few answers emerge – because the remains have been there so long, it is not possible to say if they died of natural causes or suffered violent deaths.

Freestone Hill has a national significance because it is the first place in Ireland where evidence of mining or ore prospecting from the Bronze Age has been found. The site was used again in the Iron Age and also plays a part in our more recent history. Although it is only 460 feet above sea level, it has an enchantment all of its own and, because the terrain all around it is relatively flat, it was an ideal spot from which to defend against intruders.

During the White Boys disturbances between 1700 and 1772, a prisoner from Kilkenny Gaol, John Quinn, a schoolteacher from nearby Blanchfield, was recaptured by the city garrison on the hill, where he was hiding out, for which one Michael Keogh received a reward of £50. Quinn had been incarcerated simply because he protested against paying tithes (taxes) to absentee landlords and the Protestant Church.

It is said that if a woman from the parish of Clara brings a young man up the hill for a walk, he has no chance of escaping marriage to her within a year.

Every child in the area has, at some point, climbed to
the top and marvelled at what's below, and the hawthorn at
the summit is a particular draw for people from the parish
of Clara. Your first visit to the hawthorn in the centre of
the cairn at Freestone Hill should instil an appreciation of
times past when life was all about survival, and of the little
commune that lived and died here. It is claimed by those
living close to the hill that anyone who interferes in any
way with the hawthorn will have bad luck visited upon
them. The farm on which the hill is situated is beautifully
kept with a texture of grass, even in January, of which most
landowners would be envious. And tribute must be paid
to the farmer who saved the hawthorn when it was cut by
vandals. The Heritage Council now officially protects the
tree and while it is impossible to say how long it has stood
there, conservative estimates by gardening expert Shirley
Lanigan put it at over 300 years.

Back to the geography and archaeology – there was
a community here over 2,000 years ago and outside the
ring fort there are cultivation areas and sleeping huts.
Archaeological digs also discovered pieces of everyday
pottery ware. To back up the assertion by Cóilín Ó
Drisceoil that it was a cult-type community that practised
a particular type of worship at one stage, probably around
the third or fourth centuries AD, successive archaeologists
have pointed out that the site is similar to others in south-
western Britain where shrines were built to a number of
deities.

Many international experts have wondered about the objects found on the hill. A number of Roman bronze pieces were excavated there, including a decorated brace-let, a possible buckle stud, a strip of decorated bronze and three rings, a copper coin of Constantine the Great dated to *c.* AD 337–340, iron needles, a blue-glass bracelet, two sherds of later Roman pottery and a small, polished cone. It has been argued convincingly that these finds, especially the exotic bronzes, represent votive offerings made by a community who were well versed in the ritual practices of Roman Britain, though whether they were local inhabit-ants or persons of Romano-British stock is unknown.

After performing a geophysical survey, Cóilín agreed with Barry Raftery, who carried out the definitive research on the site and asserted that it approached the status of a small defended village. The Roman pieces were found there in 1951, the first time in Ireland that such a find was made, and that makes it a most important archaeological monument.

The most revealing information on Freestone Hill, however, came from Professor Gerhard Bersu, who was a prisoner of war in Ireland during the Second World War and who carried out seminal work throughout the country in this period. His attention to detail was central to his success, and it is he who deduced from the metal finds from the hill that mining or prospecting for ore took place there.

Dunmore Cave

A seemingly never-ending silver twined cone; a hide-out for the four-times-wed Dame Alice Kyteler; investigations by the Big Fella, Michael Collins; a cat-like monster slain there by a Kilkenny female chieftain; and a visit from a popular author of his time – Dunmore Cave between Kilkenny city and Castlecomer has many stories to tell.

It was the scene of a Viking massacre – in effect an act of ethnic cleansing – chronicled in the *Annals of the Four Masters* for the year AD 928. The *Annals* say the Dublin-based Vikings responsible killed all the men they could catch, and those they could not get out were burned inside, while any youngsters found were sold as slaves in Dublin. During archaeological investigations the remains of many women and children have been found in the cave, and carbon dating has confirmed that the bodies are from the right period.

In 1999 Dunmore Cave made international headlines. A conscientious worker was cleaning up after tourists and when he shone his torch over the terrain to see if there was any rubbish lying around, a shiny object caught his eye. What he discovered there was a find of unique value.

Within months, the archaeological world was in a tizzy, and with good reason. Forget about the silver and bronze pieces and other fragments found, it was the presence of something totally unexpected that turned heads. What hit the headlines was the hint of a very expensive, rich purple-coloured dye used in a dress to which were attached a number of silver cones. It turned out to be Byzantine in origin and all of a sudden we are sailing to that place with Yeats, through his poem 'Byzantium'.

The hoard was dated thanks to the presence of several coins minted at York, in the north of England, to around AD 970, some forty years after the great slaughter at Dunmore. Wrapped in the cloth were Hacksilver (fragments of cut and bent silver items treated as bullion) and ingots, as well as conical buttons made of fine silver wire, expertly woven. The rich hoard had been concealed in a rocky cleft, deep in the cave, and the fact that it remained there suggests the owner died suddenly and could not return to claim his or her prized possessions.

The importance of this find cannot be underestimated. The largest cone, of woven silver thread, is simply delicious and is slightly bigger than a €2 coin. Last year, *The Irish Times* newspaper named it as one of the 100 most iconic objects in the history of Ireland. It has three separate strands of silver, each composed of between fifteen and eighteen wires and, thanks to the expertise of the craftsman, probably Dublin-based, it is difficult to know where one ends and another starts.

The smaller cones in the hoard have parallels in Viking burials on the Isle of Man. What were they for? Found with them was a border of silver wire to which they seem originally to have been attached. More exciting was a small, unpromising-looking remnant of textile that turned out to be, of all things, very fine, coloured silk. It seems the pieces were part of a fabulous dress with a silver-wire border and cones that functioned either as tassels or as buttons.

The Byzantine (or possibly Arab) silk itself was more valuable than all the silver ornaments put together. The dye used to colour it was either red or purple and would only have been available to the wealthiest people. If it was the latter, the dress was truly amazing: purple dye was breathtakingly expensive. Either way, the woman who wore this dress must have made a dazzling spectacle. For the display of female wealth and status in tenth-century western Europe, glamour doesn't get much more fabulous than this. Who was this woman and where did she come from? I doubt if she was from Dunmore, Muckalee, Castlecomer or the city, but was probably from some far-off land – it's more romantic and exciting to think that she was a foreigner dressed in the finest of Viking style. All we know for sure is that someone had a dress worth a king's ransom, shoved it in a crack in a cave in a moment of panic and never got to come back for it.

We know from Andy Higgins in the National Museum of Ireland that the jewellery is made of North African silver wire. Exhaustive research found that the dye was obtained from the purple murex snail, which is only found on the north coast of Africa. It took several thousand snails to produce enough dye for a garment.

Also found was a buckle and strap-end from a long-decayed leather belt, possibly worn over the beautiful murex-coloured garment, and this buckle could have been mounted with the silver ornaments retrieved. Were the coins, ingots and other objects wrapped in this garment and tied up with the belt, before being hidden in a crevice in the cave? Who knows: Dunmore might throw up more secrets in the future.

The cave itself, which boasts the largest stalagmite in Ireland (twenty-one feet high), has for many years captured the imagination of many of its visitors. The following words were written in 1825 by Kilkenny author Michael Banim and reproduced in the *Dublin Penny Journal* of 1 September 1832: 'And this is the regal fairy hall; and the peasants say that when the myriad crystallisations that hang about are, on a gala evening, illuminated and when the forever falling raindrops sparkle in the fairy light, the scene becomes too dazzling for mortal life.'

The Fairy Hall remains and it is claimed that the reason there are no stones from the partially collapsed ceiling above in the hall is that the fairies removed them to allow dancing to go ahead. At least that's what the enchanting Michael Keogh told me on a tour of the national monument.

Other visitors have been less impressed. Sir Walter Scott, the author of *Ivanhoe*, *Waverly* and *Woodstock* (not the one at Inistioge!) also visited Dunmore. His son-in-law gave this account of their trip in August 1825: 'Next morning we all went to the cave at Dunmore which is vast without dignity, and dangerous without terror – a black, slippery, dirty hole.'

Dunmore is by far the most historically significant cave on the island of Ireland, with strong links to our Celtic mythology. It was reputed to be the hiding place of Dame Alice Kyteler, who was accused of witchcraft and sentenced to death in the fourteenth century, but escaped. It is claimed that she remained in the cave until she was smuggled to New Ross to board a boat which, it is believed, took her to England.

Michael Collins sent some of his men into the cave in 1919 to check if it was suitable as a hideout for IRA men on the run from the British and if there was another way out in case the crown forces pursued them. In his memoirs, the late Judge James J. Comerford of the New York State High Court said he was among those sent to check out the place. He, Bobby Shore and five others went in with candles and, when they came out, Comerford said they had come across a large number of skeletons under a grey glass case which they believed were the remains of the tribe killed by the Vikings in the cave. What in fact he saw were wet, grey stalagmites which in the light of a penny candle probably looked glassy.

However, the most exciting episode in Dunmore's history comes from the *Book of Leinster* compiled in 1160. According to this, a fierce Amazonian-type warrior, Aithbel, killed a cat-like monster called the Luchtigern in the cave. According to the book, she also killed the entire Fomorian tribe, burned the 'seven wild men', scattered the black fleet, and hunted the red hag and drowned her in the nearby River Barrow. Of course, although related in the *Book of Leinster*, we have no way of knowing whether it's a real story or just folklore.

Today the cave has a visitor centre, excellently run, and with the temperature nine degrees centigrade all year round, 352 steps underground, it is never cold or warm.[8] There are several levels and each is covered by the dominant material of that time. As you go down the steps, the landscape changes and within a minute there is no growth and you enter another world. Some of the stalagmites look like the creature from the movie *Alien* and with carefully placed lighting it is absolutely breathtaking. It is, though, a pity there is no longer access to the blue pool in the inner chamber (the Crystal Hall), which is only reachable by sliding down the narrow entrance on your belly – no longer allowed.

The cave opened up after the ceiling collapsed about 3,500 years ago when acid-strengthened rainwater got

---

8   To get to Dunmore Cave just travel out on the Castlecomer road from Kilkenny city for four and a half miles and turn right at the well-signposted junction.

through the cracks, expanded after freezing and eventually caused the cracks to grow until such time as they could no longer hold up the huge limestone slabs. Some people, no matter how much they try to deflect attention from themselves, have a way of making life a little brighter for others. One such is Michael Keogh, tour guide extraordinaire, who has a fascination with Kilkenny history and in particular with Dunmore Cave. He tells a story that a Stone-Age farmer came out one morning to check on two goats and found them at the bottom of what was described as a 'yawning chasm'. Since then the cave has been used regularly, but never as a place of residence like the caves in southern France.

St John's Priory

Take a step back in time and imagine a magnificent enclosed forty-acre site in the middle of medieval Kilkenny with a huge priory, church, chambers and a hostel at its centre. Visualise hundreds of apprentice knights, jousting and sword fighting down to the edge of the River Nore. The young men, in the colours of their masters, would mount their steeds and speed a mile or so away to get in some archery practice by the Breagagh River; hence the name of the place, The Butts.

If you asked most people in Kilkenny where exactly the 'Lantern of Ireland' is located they would not have a clue. Yet at one time its fame was on a par with a fledgling Kilkenny Castle, it had links to the most powerful sects in the 'civilised world' and it provided soldiers for the crusades. The proper name for the establishment was St John's Priory. 'Lantern of Ireland' came from the sight of the candles in the slender, Gothic windows of the structure, a sight sadly lost to modern Ireland.

Inside the priory's magnificent remains are vaults, crypts and tombs from various ages, including the celebrated Purcell twin tomb. And there are still glimpses of what made St John's one of the most significant sites in all of Leinster outside Dublin. The heraldic arms and the ruins of the priory tiles are still there, yet everything else has been knocked down and the stone used in the surrounding buildings. St John's Church, on John Street, directly across the road from Langton's famous hotel, restaurant and theatre, was partly built from the priory's ruins.

Kells Priory, eight miles outside the city, can give us some idea of what existed at St John's Priory, although an archaeological dig has indicated that St John's was probably more sophisticated than its rural counterpart. To quote archaeologist Paul Stevens: 'chambered sandstone almost certainly represents the partially demolished remains of the late thirteenth-century Blessed Lady Chapel transept or an attached cloistral building and the presence of decorated medieval floor tiles suggests the building was richly decorated.'

St John's was an Augustinian abbey and was moved in the twelfth century from John's Bridge, where Matt the Miller's pub stands today, to its present home. For a few hundred years it was an integral part of the new city and had a massive influence on the streets that now surround it. Yet today, walking on Michael Street or Maudlin Street, it is as if the priory at St John's never existed, or, if it did, was of little note – although nothing could be further from the truth.

We know from the *Liber Primus*, Kilkenny's own version of the *Book of Kells*, that in 1220 Mass was said at the priory for the first time. The *Liber Primus* also tells us that in 1325 the building of the new house and curtilage began, leading to the priory's golden period. However, tragedy struck just four years later, when the bell tower fell during what the book describes as 'The octave of the Holy Innocents'.

Before they succumbed to all the vices that Kilkenny could offer, the monks in the priory lived by their three vows of poverty, chastity and obedience, gave hospitality to pilgrims and travellers, and tended the sick. The monks certainly started the first real mills on the Nore, including the most successful, Ormonde Mills.

We know from Fr Clohessy writing in the *Old Kilkenny Review* that there was a stream here and another one flowing through Evans Home, situated right behind the priory and the site of the first military barracks in Kilkenny, and into the River Nore at John's Quay, which was named after St John's Priory. There was a bridge on the front side of the site and the arch can still be seen, although the little tributary of the Nore it went over has long since passed underground. In a grant made by William Marshall to the priory back in 1211, mention is made of 'a certain place at the head of the small bridge of Kilkenny, to wit, that between the small aqueduct of the way that leads from my Carns to Loghmaderan, and sixteen acres of free lands on the same side of the said aqueduct with their appurtenances, to build a religious house, in honour of God and St. John, for the support of the poor and indigent'.[9] Marshall, who was married to the daughter of Richard de Clare, commonly known as Strongbow, also gave the brothers the tithes (taxes) from the mills, fisheries, orchards and dovecotes located on the forty acres of the priory site.

However, it is for its association with the brotherhood of the Knights Hospitallers of St John of Jerusalem that St John's Priory is best known. The monks provided accommodation for trainee knights and the area around St John's saw combat training of all sorts.

In 1540 the priory, along with the other monasteries, was suppressed by Henry VIII and with some of its property was transferred to the Corporation of Kilkenny. We learn from documents of that time that it was offered, with all its possessions, at a fee-farm rent of £16 6s 4d. Corporation records (located by the late Peter Farrelly) also tell us that the monastery stretched from Michael Street and Maudlin Street to the river, but in 1588 was reduced to property including 'a church, belfry and cemetery, a hall, dormitory, six chambers, a kitchen, store and granary'.

At the time the monastery was suppressed it was responsible for leasing out sixteen gardens to those living around John Street, Michael Street and Maudlin Street. Some of those gardens still exist today, but the priory was

---

9   Francis Grose, *The Antiquities of Ireland*, Vol. 1 (London, 1791), pp. 31–2.

not so lucky. During the period around the Confederation of Kilkenny, in 1645, the site was granted to the Jesuits and part of it was also occupied by the Capuchins, but Cromwell expelled the Jesuits in 1650. After the end of the Williamite Wars, both orders were expelled from Kilkenny and the site fell into ruin.

Around 1780, the nave of the main chapel, its two towers and attendant buildings were demolished. The stone was used in the construction of Evans Home, which is now being renovated and will soon be the new home of the prestigious Butler Gallery, currently situated in the basement of Kilkenny Castle. The remains of the Blessed Lady Chapel of the priory (*c.* 1290) survive and were incorporated into the present Protestant St John's Church in 1817. To the rear of Evans Home a small fragment of cloistral building with vaulting survives within the western boundary wall.

The Church of Ireland is very accommodating about letting people into the priory ruins behind the church that is still in use today. The light of St John's, once the Lantern of Ireland, may be quenched, but it still casts a long shadow through the city. So the next time you walk past St John's Church, just look in and to the left, and study the high arches of what was once a proud and prestigious establishment that had links with continental Europe. Like many of our hidden gems it begs more questions than it answers and certainly hasn't received the recognition it deserves.

Mount Loftus

The enthralling and engaging memoir of Bettina Grattan-Bellew on a place called Mount Loftus, roughly equidistant from Goresbridge, Graignamanagh, Borris and Gowran, is the Irish equivalent of Margaret Mitchell's masterpiece *Gone with the Wind*. The house is immediately recognisable because of its wonderful entrance, designed in the nineteenth century by William Turner. Bettina, the eldest daughter of Major John E. B. Loftus and his wife Pauline, inherited Mount Loftus after her brother died at the age of twenty-two. Her 1964 article in the *Old Kilkenny Review* might do little to change our stereotypical view of the landed gentry, who received huge tracts of land in Ireland and enjoyed lives of pure indulgence, but it allows us to empathise with them.

The story of the Loftus family is one of integration and how the local people around Powerstown, Skeoughvosteen and communities in the vicinity of Mount Loftus came to respect them and their links with the area, deepened after so many 'natural' children were conceived with local women. The testosterone-filled men of Mount Loftus looked after their offspring, and loyalty towards the Loftus clan remained strong. Was their way of life a more natural existence than the downtrodden Catholic way of doing things at that time?

By far the most colourful, randy, unashamedly amoral and drink-loving, gambling reprobate of them all was Sir Nicholas Loftus. He must have been a fantastic character and people still talk about him. We will dwell on him later, with his famous racehorses and his women.

Tragedy has been part and parcel of Mount Loftus too. During the 1798 rising, a daughter of Sir Edward Loftus, who was high sheriff (the king's representative in Kilkenny), had her life shattered in an instant. Her father was tipped off in advance of the rising by being warned that 'the climate of Mount Loftus might not suit him'. He had Elizabeth and her mother taken to Wexford, but as their carriage was going into the town, the girl saw the head of her lover, Bagenal Harvey, stuck on a pike on the bridge. Although her family were the English monarch's representatives, he had been a United Irishman.

The United Irishmen drank out the cellar when they entered Mount Loftus, but they did not burn it to the ground or ransack it as happened at other places, and the reason might have been their knowledge of the high sheriff's great regard for Napper Tandy, one of the leaders of the revolt. Or was it because Sir Edward was hedging his bets in case the struggle for Irish freedom was successful? It would seem so from letters in possession of the Loftus family, in which he was communicating with leaders of the revolt and leading Catholic churchmen of the time.

Elizabeth Loftus never married and spent the rest of her life with her two brothers at the estate, which at one time covered over 4,000 acres, although from the 1800s until Ireland gained its independence in 1922 it was around 2,000 acres.

Although the Loftus name has long since disappeared from here, the family's colourful reputation continues to flourish. It all started when Mount Loftus and the entire estate was won, in 1752, by a member of the Loftus family in a card game at the original Loftus residence in Ireland, the haunted Loftus Hall near Hook Head, County Wexford. The unfortunate loser of the card game, John Eaton of Cromwellian-settler extraction, stubbornly refused to quit the Kilkenny property. In his doomed efforts to keep the estate he employed two prize fighters, one armed with a pike and the other with a blunderbuss, who never left his side so that he could not be served with the legal writ. The law has long been changed and gambling debts are now unenforceable in law.

In her article for the *Old Kilkenny Review*, Bettina Grattan-Bellew speaks with great warmth about Sir Nicholas (1763–1832), who had a new house built in 1769:

> Here is one of his love stories. One day he was walking in the Barracks in Kilkenny when he saw one of his sergeants beating and abusing his wife. The wife was an extremely good-looking woman but her husband did not seem to

appreciate her properly. Sir Nicholas was touched. He had an eye for beauty and especially for beauty in distress. He bought the woman from her husband there and then and took her to Mount Loftus, where he installed her in a house called Whalebone Hall near the present walled garden and he was wont to say he was never so happy as when he was in the arms of his mistress with his favourite racer neighing in his box below.

The most famous Sir Nick story tells how, coming back to Mount Loftus one day, he met a hawker selling whip handles made from holly. Sir Nicholas spotted a young horse behind the hawker's cart and, being a good judge of horses, bought him for £5. He turned out to be the finest racehorse of his day and was called Hollyhock (whip handle). He won fifteen King's Plates, was unbeatable in England and Ireland, and is buried at Mount Loftus.

In 1864 the unmarried Elizabeth Loftus, who had outlived her brothers, died and left Loftus Hall to Mary Murphy. Mary, however, was a Catholic. Her father was Edward Loftus, Elizabeth's younger brother and a British Army officer killed in foreign lands, while her mother was Mary Carroll, the daughter of a local Catholic farmer tenant. The local Protestant clergyman and his wife, distant relations of the Loftus family, took a legal action stating that Mary Murphy was illegitimate and couldn't succeed to the property according to the Penal Laws. These had been introduced to ensure Catholics obtained no legal title

Ballyspellan Spa. Once famed throughout Ireland, Britain and the Continent for the healing qualities of its water, it now lies in ruins and is forgotten by most. *Courtesy of Eoin Hennessy*

The Ballyspellan Brooch. This priceless piece was found in a field in 1806. A replica was presented to Queen Victoria by Prince Albert at Christmas 1849. *Courtesy of the National Museum of Ireland*

Part of the grounds of Woodstock, developed by the Tighe family into a place of beauty, looking towards the River Nore. *Author's collection*

Danesfort Turret. A hunting folly built by the Wemys family who used to shoot deer from the first floor as their servants drove the animals past the turret. *Courtesy of Eoin Hennessy*

Knockroe Passage Tomb. Still used for pagan worship, it is aligned with the winter solstice and is well known for its extensive assemblage of megalithic art. *Courtesy of the Kilkenny People*

Kilcreene Lodge. Home to the Smithwick brewing family for generations, it is within a stone's throw of Kilkenny city centre, yet is completely serene. *Courtesy of Michael Brophy*

Grennan Castle. Situated on the River Nore in Thomastown, it is closely associated with the Denn family. *Courtesy of Dylan Vaughan*

Dunmore Cave, where, in 1999, the discovery of a hoard of silver cones and other metals dating from AD 970 associated with a dress created an international flurry among archaeologists. *Courtesy of Michael Keogh*

Mount Loftus House. Home to the amorous Loftus men, the estate was won by the family in a card game in 1752. *Courtesy of Michael Brophy*

Leac an Scailc. The largest dolmen in Ireland. *Courtesy of Eoin Hennessy*

Rossenarra House. Boasting former guests like Frank Sinatra, and with direct connections to four US presidents, it was also once home to the great portrait painter, Lord Lavery. *Author's collection*

The Bishop's Palace. Situated on the most ancient site in Kilkenny city and the former home of the Church of Ireland Bishops of Ossory, it is now home to The Heritage Council. *Courtesy of Eoin Hennessy*

Tybroughney Castle. Surrounded by a mass of significant archaeological sites, Tybroughney is owned and lived in by the Dowley family, who are restoring it to its former greatness.
Courtesy of Joe Cashin

The haunting stained glass window at Ballybur Castle by Shane Grincell.
Courtesy of Eoin Hennessy

The Long Gallery, Kilkenny Castle. The ceiling in the Long Gallery
contains one of the most important artistic creations in Ireland.
Courtesy of the Office of Public Works

St Canice's Cathedral, an iconic sight of Kilkenny city.
Courtesy of Elizabeth Keys, administrator, St Canice's Cathedral

to property, among other things, but they were beginning to lose their hold by this time. The clergyman lost the case and, according to Bettina, well-wishers swamped Mary Murphy when the train carrying her from Dublin finally arrived at Goresbridge Station.

Many people have wondered why the old stately home at Mount Loftus was knocked down at the turn of the last century. The answer is simple – Bettina's father, Captain John Edward Blake Loftus, took over the run-down house minus the estate in 1903, having repurchased it through the high court after debts mounted and couldn't be paid. He married Pauline May Lichtenstadt, only daughter of August Lichtenstadt of Seymour Street, London. She was unhappy with the old house, which was more or less falling down, and insisted that a new one be constructed to her tastes. It was completed in 1909.

All through the piece in the *Old Kilkenny Review*, Bettina shows a kindness in her writing that humanises the Loftus family. She died in 1995 and the house was sold because her two children lived abroad. Her husband was Thomas Henry (Hal) Grattan-Bellew, a great-great-grandson of Henry Grattan, the famous Irish patriot who spent his life fighting for Catholic Emancipation. This may explain why two of Grattan's banners calling for free trade and legislative rights for the Irish parliament ended up at Mount Loftus and were sold by those doyens of Great House sales, The Mealy's of Castlecomer, when the estate was sold.

As you walk up the avenue to Mount Loftus, on the left is what remains of Dromroe Castle, the name meaning russet or yellow ridge. In 1525 Charles Kavanagh, son of Maurice the Younger, his mother and nine others were burned to death at Dromroe in a deliberate attack by a rival chieftain. Wouldn't you know, superstition has it that the ghosts of those who died walk Mount Loftus at night. The castle, it is said, was doomed from the start because it was erected on a rath. It seems that in the nineteenth century it was used as a dovecote for pigeons that ferried messages between the great houses of the region, or was just there to fatten the tasty birds.

Thankfully, today, Mount Loftus is an absolutely glorious place to visit thanks to owners Pat and Bridget Byrne who have done so much to enhance it. The house is wonderful and so tastefully in keeping with the original that to the untrained eye it looks 300 years old. The front pillars of the house are from the original structure.

The Byrnes have managed to retain the original atmosphere of the place as well. As Bridget said: 'If you can't find peace at Mount Loftus, you won't be able to find it anywhere.' The love of horses has also continued and Pat has enjoyed great success with them, especially Quyinze, which won the Galway Hurdle in 1999 when trained by local man Pat Hughes. He has won a total of sixteen races and been placed a further nine times.

The present Mount Loftus is the third on that spot and we hope that the Byrnes, with their warm hospitality and love of the place, long continue for many years to come. They have done an invaluable service to the county in retaining the essence of Mount Loftus – benevolence.

Cushendale Woollen Mills

Cushendale Woollen Mills is the only surviving woollen mill in the south-east of Ireland. The current custodian of the mill is passionate about his craft. When Philip Cushen was just nineteen years old his father Patrick passed away, leaving the young man to manage one of the most important craft industries in Graignamanagh. An iconic brand, it has survived in some form or other since a group of English monks founded Duiske Abbey 800 years ago and set up their own mill on the present site of Cushendale. They produced lambswool and what wasn't used for their own clothing was given to the poor and the rest exported.

The sixth generation of his family to run Cushendale Woollen Mills, Philip has managed to safeguard the future by investing in new ideas and new concepts while remaining true to the way in which the clothes and other wool, lambswool and mohair items are produced. You can feel the sense of history, place and the past as you enter the building. It is the last mill of its type in the city and county to have survived; many people in Kilkenny will remember Greenvale and Ormonde Mills, which were great employers but are, alas, long since extinct.

The plain exterior of the building does not prepare you for the richness and diversity of what is inside. The old mill, once powered by the mill stream, diverted from the Duiske River with its source on Brandon Hill, is full of character. All the machines still work perfectly; some are now used to carry out processes for other Irish woollen manufacturers who long ago dispensed with theirs, only to find they still needed them. Cushendale is a special place, to be guarded and cherished, where a man, proud of his craft and its link with its surroundings, puts quality before quantity as he deals with changing production methods and consumer demands.

Many of his fellow weavers have given up and are 'outsourcing'. It may be a good short-term idea, but in the long term it will mean that certain skills and ways of doing things, passed down through generations, will be lost because the next generation will not have the knowledge, and then we will be dependent on imports – which will make our Irish-produced items extinct. 'They will never produce anything again, that's it,' Philip Cushen said with authority and a hint of sadness. He has got soul, real soul, and is passionate about yarns, wool, mohair and keeping alive a way of life, a craft/art form which has been going on around the town of Graignamanagh since the thirteenth century. The building on the Mill Road, backing onto the River Duiske, provides the town with a sense of identity which is almost as important as Duiske Abbey.

The part played by the River Duiske in providing a

clean water source is highlighted by Philip, who explains that, unlike over 55 per cent of water supplies in Kilkenny which come through limestone, making the water 'hard', water in the Duiske comes through, or down from, Brandon Hill, which is the final granite outcrop of the mountains ranging from south of Dublin to South Leinster – this gives the water a purity and a softness which are extremely important in the textile milling industry. The water is also used by many families for drinking and it certainly tastes pure.

Philip can trace his weaving heritage all the way back to the Flemish artisans who fled mainland Europe in the mid-1600s and came to the south-east of Ireland. Indeed, he still uses some of the Flemish words brought over all those centuries ago – like 'stok', a length of cloth, and 'skerrin', the frame on which yarn is placed in preparation for weaving.

He is a lover of language and 'dabbles' in many of the European ones, being interested especially in the Celtic tongues. His energy is palpable and it transmits to those who work with him and have the same passion for the business that he has. You also sense that he has a healthy disregard for those who say there is no future for the textile industry in Ireland. He rubbishes that idea, and says that working with wool, weaving and doing other things to the fabrics involved has an artistic side that defines who we are, and this is worth preserving.

Though the creation of the rich colours and designs

associated with Cushendale is a matter of chemistry, the making of the actual fabric is today a mechanical process. Philip asks where else you would find such diversity of challenges in the one job. He wants to find new ways of working with existing fabric to create new lines and breathe new life into the textiles industry to ensure its survival.

For Philip it is all about history, dedication and maintaining a way of life that is quickly becoming extinct on these shores. When his grandfather was in business, he produced blankets for the local market and was able to make a living so doing:

> My grandfather Philip depended on the people of Graignamanagh for his livelihood. My father had to expand and depended on the markets in Cork, Dublin and especially Waterford for business, while I have had to go global, selling to buyers in the US, France, Germany and Japan. However, the Irish at home and abroad continue to be our most important customers and this is more than ever the case during these tough economic times when people are coming to recognise and value indigenous Irish crafts.

Philip has embraced new technology and is selling all over the world thanks to his website.

Having finished secondary school, Philip was supposed to go to a textile college in the south of Scotland, but his father's premature death put an end to that. He lost his father's guidance and secrets of the craft overnight. It cost him and he feels that he wasted over ten years figuring out things for himself, things he could have learned in college in a few years. He is philosophical about it, and the fact that he had to graft so hard to learn and to keep up with the rest of those in the industry has stood to him and given him an independence that he might not otherwise have gained, and which now gives him an edge over competitors. However, he did receive a boost with the establishment of the Kilkenny Design Workshops in the late 1960s, set up to help the craft industry locally and nationally. He recalls with gratitude Kerryman Mortimer O'Shea being in charge of the textile part of the workshops. 'Working there with those professionals gave me an insight into design and products which I would not have otherwise got,' Philip explains. Luckily for him it also stimulated an awareness of old designs which have now been revitalised, and Cushendale was and is able to capitalise on that.

Philip is great with his hands: he has no choice, because many of the machines are complex and repairing them requires an intuitive knowledge of mechanics. Not surprisingly, two of his sons are mechanical engineers. Patrick works on pharmaceutical product lines while Philip Jnr, who lives in Belgium, works with Toyota. The youngest member of the family, Michael, works with a mapping firm in Dublin. Philip Senior and his wife Mary, who also works in the mills, also have four daughters. Both

Anna Maria and Ellen are pharmacists based in Dublin, while Breda is a doctor working at present in Galway. Miriam works in human resources. It continues to be a strong family business with Miriam, Michael and Patrick actively involved. Although he does not dare say it, you can see that Philip would be proud if any of them showed a willingness to follow him into what is a sometimes perilous but very fulfilling walk of life, some would say a vocation.

At present the Cushendale Woollen Mills range includes blankets, throws for lounges and bedrooms, travel rugs, and other fabrics used in homes and hotel interiors. Its home furnishings come in a range of fibres, colours and sizes: mohair (brushed and bouclé), 100 per cent Irish wool, lambswool and cotton chenille. There are scarves, hats, ruanas (capes), pocket stoles and other fashion items. Recently the business has expanded into supplying the handcrafts sector with knitting and crochet yarns and felting wools.

Philip Cushen has a great respect for the past and for those who went before him. He has noticed that as time goes on he is selling more and more to people who can recognise and appreciate the value of a quality product and the story that goes with it. People want to buy something unique that will last and that looks different, distinctive and is made by hand in Graignamanagh.

Philip has a fire that burns bright to produce things of beauty and excellence. 'You are always trying to make something better than the last product, to set a higher standard,' he explained. 'You must be fired up enough to always try to create something different, unique, something of which you can be proud,' he added. Noble words from a man who is keeping alive a tradition which has an important place in our history and hopefully a place in our future.

Leac an Scailc

Standing a staggering eighteen feet high, Leac an Scailc elicits a gasp from unsuspecting visitors when they walk down from the public road, turn the corner of the hedgerow and see it for the first time. Ireland's tallest dolmen is situated in the rolling hills between Mullinavat and Piltown, and should be a jewel in the heritage of Kilkenny. Yet, the mystical tomb of the warrior/hero (Leac an Scailc), also known as Kilmogue Dolmen, is by and large forgotten. This isn't helped by the misleading signposts, some of which even say Harristown Dolmen when it is obvious to everyone that it is in the townland of Kilmogue.

Before we delve into the story of Leac an Scailc, two really positive aspects to my visit to the site one Wednesday morning should be related. A few hundred yards away, and just a stone's throw from a place known locally as Ashtown, double All-Ireland senior hurling medal winner Liam McCarthy was busy making hurleys from locally grown ash, preserving another hugely important part of our heritage. The other was that an archaeology student from University College Dublin was doing research for her thesis on prehistoric burial places along the Suir Valley.

She was investigating the micro-lines on these stones, made of quartz (white marble-like blooded nuggets embedded in the stones), and exploring whether they formed part of the worship of old deities. Who knows, we might finally see a first ever excavation of the site which boasts such a magnificent reminder of our past.

Leac an Scailc doesn't feature on our famed tourist trail and no coach tours stop there. This doesn't discourage Germans, English and other foreign visitors from coming to see this man-made structure and marvelling how, without pulleys or JCBs, our ancestors managed to place such huge boulders on top of each other to create a mystical place which has enthralled civilisations during the 5,000 or more years it has been there. Despite the challenges posed by the lack of accurate signposts, these tourists still manage to find what is for them a magnetic place, where you can touch history and get a feeling of what our first ancestors were all about and how they honoured their dead.

I also wonder if these dolmens served another purpose. We don't know for certain, but they seem, in the case of South Kilkenny at least, to have been placed strategically, and if you could take away the ditches, boundaries, bungalows and plantations of coniferous trees that are there now, and have an unobstructed view of these monuments, it would be possible to get some sense of their dominance in the landscape. As they commanded views of huge areas of the surrounding countryside, is it possible that they were used as lookout posts along the valleys they populate?

Taken in isolation Leac an Scailc is an oddity, but when taken in tandem with all the other tombs (Raheen, Knockroe and Kilmacoliver), all the pre-Christian standing stones and other Neolithic remains in the immediate area, it seems to have far more significance; yet no one has so far put their finger on how precisely these monuments are related. With just a little imagination, you can visualise Leac an Scailc being the only large structure visible on the horizon. Now, nestled in between the border of the fields and with part of its structure used as a boundary, it is no longer visible from the road or from Corbally Woods, a few miles below on the other side of the valley, or above from Kingsmountain or Booleyglass Hill.

It should be mandatory for every schoolchild in Kilkenny to be brought here to heighten their awareness of our past. The sheer size of the portal tomb is amazing, and the engineering that went into putting a large granite capstone, resting on two equally large stones with a pillow stone resting on a back stone for extra stability, is equally enthralling. The stones at the base are around twelve feet high and the capstone reaches eighteen feet. The entrance faces north-east, away from the prevailing wind, and it has an enormous doorstone almost ten feet high.

In mid-morning the sun catches the side of the dolmen and it looks majestic with an unnamed tributary of the Poulanassa River trickling next to it and eventually finding its way into the River Suir. And as you stand there, you realise that whatever the real use of this huge piece, it had a relevance and importance to the people who built it and who obviously came to worship at it or to pay homage to their dead, probably their chiefs.

The OPW has put up a little plaque telling everyone that the monument is in its care. What the little sign doesn't tell you is that Leac an Scailc is at the heart of an area with almost the same concentration of ancient chambers, and other archaeological and historical gems, as Newgrange or the Hill of Tara, yet it is left relatively untapped as a resource on which to build our understanding of our predecessors and on which to develop a heritage tourist trail. No words can adequately describe the impact it has on you when you first see it. Yet it is now hidden between two fields with bushes and undergrowth continually threatening to claim it.

It is a fantastical place and begs more questions than it answers. We can be sure that the people who built it were our first farmers, and carved patches out of the forests. But who were they? We are told that the first people to come to Ireland, when the ice had melted, were hunter-gatherers, who, having crossed from Scandinavia to Britain around 6000 BC or earlier, moved first into Antrim and Wicklow and then down into Kilkenny. Growing evidence from DNA gathering, however, suggests they came not from Scandinavia, but from North Africa. We know little about these middle-Stone Age or Mesolithic people whose funerary monuments – portal tombs, court-tombs, wedge-tombs and passage tombs – dot the countryside. But despite this lack of knowledge about its builders, which will hopefully be rectified in the future as more data becomes available, if you are in Kilkenny you should visit Leac an Scailc – you won't be disappointed.

Rossenarra House

E ven by Kilkenny standards, Rossenarra House just outside Kilmoganny has a pedigree that is stunning. Magical is the only word to describe the landscape that hits you when you look out from the front of the house at the rich Kilkenny landscape that stretches for miles and miles in front of you like a carpet.[10] On a clear night you can see the village of Stradbally, County Laois, as the landscape unfolds before you, with a pattern being made by the lights of Dunamaggin, Kells, Callan, Bennettsbridge and Kilkenny city. It remains a favourite part of the world for moonlighting couples who sit in their car looking down on the wonderful view.

The house itself has associations with four US presidents and was designed by the Irish-born architect James Hoban, who was also responsible for the White House. Film stars and rock stars mixed here with the country's elite. This country's greatest portrait painter, Sir John Lavery, whose portrait of his wife adorned our

---

10 To get to Rossenarra go to the village of Kells, and from there go with the turn on the road to the village of Kilmoganny. In the centre of Kilmoganny, turn left and then immediately right. Two miles further is Rossenarra.

currency for years, died here. Throw in hydropower and the self-sufficient McEnery family who lived in the house and who bred the greatest Grand National horse of all time, Red Rum, and you have a true story that borders on fantasy.

Rossenarra House, with its five bays and three storeys over a huge basement, was designed around 1824–25 in the Palladian style, having been commissioned by Maurice Reade who owned Castle Howell and the thousands of acres around it. Castle Howell, the original Walsh clan stronghold, was located a few fields away from Rossenarra. Today on the Kyle to Kilmoganny road you can still see the two sets of gates and one lodge where the titled people entered in their carriages on their way to the house to be entertained by Reade, who was the leader of the Walsh clan, members of which were very numerous in the area.

The obituary of an early owner of Rossenarra, Mr William Morris Reade, from *The Kilkenny Journal* of 31 March 1847, gives a wonderful sense of the times:

> It is with much more than ordinary feelings of sorrow and regret that we have this day to announce a great public calamity which has fallen on this county by the unexpected death of a gentleman whose sterling worth and high standing was second to that of no landed proprietor in Ireland. We have to record the demise of William Morris Reade Esq on Wednesday last of fever, at his seat, Rossenarra, a gentleman whose usefulness and virtue it needs no comment of ours to make known to this

community, in whose individual breasts his excellent qualities and worth will be responded to and acknowledged, and his loss unfeignedly deplored. As a country gentleman he was a perfect and finished model, uniting the sister virtues of courtesy and hospitality; extending around his demesne an unostentatious but richly beneficent charity, the termination of which by his premature death will be bitterly and poignantly felt. As a magistrate, he was active and energetic in the discharge of his duties, and unceasing in his efforts to prevent crime in its first budding, or detect and punish it in a developed state – at the same time, on all occasions, tempering justice with mercy. As a landlord, he was resident, in the best sense of the word, attending unremittingly to the comforts of his tenants, whose condition he so far ameliorated that their present state presents a marked oasis in the desert of Irish misery, apathy and neglect. In politics Mr Reade was an unflinching and uncompromising Conservative, sticking to the good cause through weal and woe, and despising the time-serving policy of some of those who unjustly boast of the name; but his private worth and sterling honesty of purpose was acknowledged by all sections of politics and all denominations of religion. In recording the death of such a man as this, it is our wish to avoid the common and hackneyed expression of grief, which the departure of ordinary mortals calls forth. Mr Reade was truly one man in a thousand, and never was a time-honoured quotation more aptly applied than to record of him the honest truth. 'We ne'er shall look upon his like again.' The demise of this exemplary gentleman is the more melancholy and to be 'lamented', as it is feared and believed he contracted the fever which was its cause, in his efforts to detect the murderers of the late Mr Prim; it being at least a fact that he entered and closely searched one suspect house where a family was lying ill of that now most prevalent and fatal disease.

High praise indeed.

The estate passed through several generations of the Reade family until the 1880s, when it came into the possession of the McEnery family. Sir John Lavery was related to that family through marriage and he resided at Rossenarra during the last few years of his life, dying there in January 1941. It is interesting that during the negotiations to form the Free State, Michael Collins and the Irish delegation stayed at the Lavery's palatial home in London's South Kensington, and in 1999 a letter written by Lady Lavery was found describing Michael Collins as a man of 'brilliancy as a romantic figure' and praising him for his 'dignity, pride, wisdom, a wonderful beauty of character and qualities of statesmanship that only a few had begun to recognise'. She added: 'It is my greatest wish that something should be written about Michael that will be worthy of his greatness of mind and soul and that will show the world in the future, just what he meant in his life and death to the Irish people.'

After the death of the great John McEnery in the 1950s, the property of 1,700 acres was carved up by the Land Commission. Charles Cummins, who farms adjacent to Rossenarra, recalls that his father, Roger, had the house for a very short while after the Land Commission divided up the land. Dissolved around thirty years ago, the commission was created in 1881 as the body responsible for re-distributing farmland in the country. Roger sold the house to a kind Englishman, Stephen Edwards, who lived there for a short while and drank in the lovely and homely Dunphy's pub, down the road in Kilmoganny. Edwards then sold it on to Richard Condon in the 1970s.

Condon wrote *The Manchurian Candidate*, which was turned into a film starring Frank Sinatra. He had also worked on the PR for a film starring Sinatra and Sophia Loren in Spain and had struck up a friendship with Old Blue Eyes. People who live around Rossenarra found the Condons warm and friendly. And when one of the neighbours had a fire in the house they came up to help, bringing sandwiches and drink. They left, it is said, out of frustration with the telephone system. Condon would be researching something in Australia and there would be no phone lines available when he needed them because of the time-zone difference.

There are people around Kilmoganny who can go back eighty years to when the house was owned by the McEnery family, now living close by in Kells. When these pensioners look back at the history of the house, there are two names that stand out for them: Walter Griffith and his Carlow-born wife, Christine. They still talk about the parties, dinners and suppers, and how everyone in the locality was invited to mingle with the likes of Judge Peter Smithwick, Captain Blunden from Castle Blunden, Baron Brian de Breffny of

Castletown Cox and Lady Miranda Iveagh among others. It was a wonderful time and the McEnerys were delighted when Walter Griffith bought the house in a private deal from his friend Richard Condon, because they knew that he would look after it.

Coincidences abound at Rossenarra: Walter Griffith visited the White House on a number of occasions, as did Sinatra and Richard Condon. And the association doesn't stop there. One of the Morris-Reades, a relative of the current president of the US, Barack Obama, has owned the place as well.

I am indebted to the late Alice McEnery-Gwynn for her account of her life at Rossenarra from the *Old Kilkenny Review* of 1983. She explains how the family had everything they ever needed while at Rossenarra, including their own water turbine which supplied them with free electricity. I am glad to say that her son, Martin McEnery, who ran the place for a short while after his father John's death, is still alive and living in Kells.

Sadly this once great house now looks a little run down: the entrance is overgrown and the windowsills on the outside need a lot of work. The current owner, Denis O'Sullivan, bought it twelve years ago from the Griffith family, and it has not been lived in on a permanent basis since then, although there have been a number of caretakers. Rossenarra needs attention, but during the current economic climate it doesn't seem likely that will happen any time soon.

A trio of treasures at Kilree

Kells just oozes heritage. It is laden with jewels from our past, and while most people are immediately drawn to Kells Priory, one of the largest and best-preserved walled monastic sites in Europe, there is another, more mystical place that is just as important in the parish. Its history stretches back further than the Augustinian brotherhood of the priory, and it is a place where you have to beware of the bull and where, when the wind blows, you feel as if you are under a spell.

At Kilree there is a trio of treasures – a round tower, an ancient church and a high cross where a king may or may not be buried. Adding to the mystique is a fourth, natural phenomenon, a bullaun (hollow) stone that was used by the first inhabitants of this island to drink from and, we think, to practise pagan idolatry. When you first view Kilree coming from the hill on the far side of Kells village it reminds you of Freestone Hill – an ancient place used before Christianity. Kilree has commanding views of the surrounding countryside and seems to be the highest spot in the area and, therefore, a natural stronghold. Looking from it, you take in Knockdrinnagh Wood, Ballygowan (the original home of the water with the same name),

Hugginstown and the high lands beyond it, and around to the Slieveardagh Hills. It also boasts views of Slievenamon and the Comeraghs.

So it begs the question: was the ancient round tower of Kilree used as a lookout, with domed bells on top sounded when danger was imminent? Did it continue in use as a lookout in the thirteenth, fourteenth and fifteenth centuries? This is probably too simplistic a view, but we are sure of one thing – the tower was built around the eleventh century and would have been used as a defence against the marauding Vikings who had a stronghold in Waterford and at Grannagh, upriver on the Suir in the south of the county of Kilkenny.

It is said, but not proven, that the bones of a great king are buried under the high cross at Kilree, just forty yards from the round tower and the Church of St Brigid that lies in ruins, yet is still a strong draw for the people of the area from Kells and Stoneyford. Up to the middle of the nineteenth century it was claimed that King Niall Caille was buried here in AD 844 and that his bones lay under the high cross which is uninscribed. It seems now that the high cross was erected well before that date and we learn from different researchers that these kinds of crosses were commemorative and not built to cover the dead.

Although it stands ninety feet high, Kilree round tower is not easy to see because it is set amid tall trees. As it is a fine, slim construction, with a diameter inside of just nine feet, it must have been tight in there. With six different levels and a battlement area at the top as well as a belfry, it is little wonder that rope ladders were used. As with the other round towers in the county, the entrance faces the church. The round tower and church are enclosed in a grove of beautiful deciduous trees, and once you enter this wonderful place you can feel the past coming at you. A sign in bold yellow at the entrance tells you to beware of the bull. Don't be put off; I have never seen one there. The land is extremely fertile and there is a rich covering of spring grass on the field.

It is important to appreciate the work done by researchers over the years on Kilree and the rest of the county: Canon Carrigan's *History of the Diocese of Ossory*; the wonderful parish history of Dunamaggin by Richard Lahart, which provides us with so much detail about the area; and especially the findings of Ireland's great antiquarian scholar from Slieverue in South Kilkenny, John O'Donovan, which are probably the most revealing. O'Donovan's research on place names and on sites like Kilree for the Ordnance Survey is invaluable in deepening our knowledge of our past. He upset a lot of people when he said the real ancient Irish name for the site was not actually Kilree, which up to then had been taken to mean the church of the king, Niall Caille. Instead he claimed it was Cill Freach, named for a female saint, Freach. Canon Carrigan also studied this, and he felt that Kilree was a corruption of the name Cill Ruiddchi, the Church of St Ruiddchi. While it is hard to be sure of the original name of the church, Cill Bride seems to be the most plausible. We know from local people and from Richard Lahart that the well at Kilree was named in honour of St Brigid and that it dates back over 1,000 years. It is hard to ignore Cill an Rí as the root of the name of the site, and of course the round tower is still known locally by people as The Steeple, a reference to the bell tower at the top of it.

Only the outer walls remain of the church, but inside the tombs of local people tell you that some of them, at least, were well off. The poorer people would have been buried furthest away from the church. From Norman times the Howlings, Holdens or Howels are associated with the site. From medieval times, the Comerfords were closely associated with Kilree, along with the Izod, Fleming, Ryan and St Leger families, and, of course, in recent times, the Goreys, who represented Kilkenny in Dáil Éireann.

What stands out most about Kilree is that it is still used as a graveyard and the ancient burial ground is well looked after by the people living in the area. While you may think you are alone when visiting, there is nearly always someone keeping a watchful eye over the place, and that's reassuring.

The bullaun stone is located 250 yards north of the round tower in the corner of a field of heavily weathered limestone and is marked on the Ordnance Survey map for the area. Local folklore often attaches religious or magical significance to bullaun stones, such as the belief that the rainwater collecting in the stone's hollow has healing properties. Ritual use of some bullaun stones continued well into the Christian period and many are found in association with early churches such as Kilree (or should that be St Brigid's or St Freach's or St Ruiddchi's – take your pick).

Again the lack of signposts for such an amazing place is sad. The only sign coming from Kilkenny city is at Kells Priory, which is a wonderful place to visit but it doesn't have the *draíocht* of Kilree.

St Francis Abbey Brewery

W hat comes to mind when you think of the St Francis Abbey Brewery, or, to give it the name by which most local people know it, Smithwick's Brewery? Is it the smell of malting barley, lightly heated before machination, allied with the scent of hops from later in the brewing process which permeates the air? Or the iconic old entrance at The Ring (Parliament Street) where you can still see the cobbles over which horse-led drays made their way in and out of this sacred place? Older citizens will think of Walter Smithwick with his PR guru Bill Finnegan who, along with the independently outspoken Mick McGuinness and others, brought the Munich beer festival to the city complete with tents and fräuleins and unprecedented numbers of people. In the end this event became a victim of its own success because the crowds grew too big.

When I think of the brewery it is the presence there of The Liberator, Daniel O'Connell, that comes to mind. He stayed in The Ring and addressed a huge crowd from the top window of Edmond Smithwick's living quarters, speaking about nationalism, emancipation and freedom. Smithwick called one of his sons after O'Connell and the

O'Connell papers belonging to the Smithwick family are a must-read for anyone interested in the birth of our nation. I also think of the soup kitchens set up by the Smithwick family during the famine. And I also think of the other great brewing family of our nation, the Guinnesses, who having purchased the brewery from the Smithwick family spent millions of pounds revitalising it. I think of the current Lord Iveagh, Ned Guinness, bringing his pals to the brewery recently for artist Mungo McGosh's bachelor party, complete with huge Nebuchadnezzars of champagne. More importantly I think of every single voluntary and sporting organisation that has had a launch or fund-raiser in the Cellar Bar and how much the brewery gives back to the city.

I think of the first monks who brewed beer that was described in records of the time as a 'fulsome brew' from a sacred well (now under one of the modern buildings); of the huge positive impact they had on the city; and of how they worked their magic in the light of a mesmerising seven-lancet window with glass made on site by Italian craftsmen. And I think of Corkonian Ian Hamilton, who has done so much to revitalise the place, but who will be the last in a long line of distinguished master brewers. But most of all I think of a magnificent twenty-five acre site, fronting on to the River Nore, which once employed 300 people and was the pulse of this city, and which must be an integral part of any master plan to regenerate the area and tie it in with the new bridge that will run through the site.

One remaining treasure is the Cellar Bar, and if you are fortunate enough to be given a tour of the brewery by Ronan Morrissey, then your appreciation of the place will be heightened immeasurably. The Cellar Bar is the best place in the world, outside a certain pub in Listowel, to drink Smithwick's. It is located thirteen feet underground and was originally used to mature the wooden beer kegs because the temperature and air pressure there are constant all year round, which led to an even and consistent flavour in the ale. The ceilings and walls are filled with different pieces of brewing memorabilia and its arched tunnel-like design seems to lend itself to the almost theatrical atmosphere.

At the end of 2013 the curtain will fall on over 600 years of brewing tradition and while there are rumours that outside interests are looking for a site on Parliament Street for a micro-brewery, we all hope that the Cellar Bar will continue in its present capacity. The fact that the twenty-five acre site has been purchased by the city and will be used for the benefit of the people of the city is a good sign. The Cellar Bar is an institution and if it isn't a listed building it should be immediately added to the register. To walk down the stairs from the Parliament Street entrance fills you with anticipation and when you enter you are not disappointed. Come next year, gone will be the smell of the hops and malted barley along with the huge trucks trundling through the city centre. There will also be a reduction in the use of the city's water supply because the brewery is by far its biggest user. Gone too will be the huge general-purpose metal vessels which can hold up to one million pints of beer each and which reach skyward like something out of the NASA complex in Florida.

The tour of the brewery provides an informative hour and a half. The knowledge of the brewing process and the history of all facets of brewery life that are imparted is incredible. And at the end of the tour the seemingly endless wait for the sample as it is pulled expertly: the roll of the glass as the ruby-red beer descends from the tap; the placing of it gently on the counter to let it 'settle' for around twenty seconds; lifting it again and rolling the glass over and over as the liquid comes out. Eventually the pint is full and after a further period of settling it is ready to consume: at this stage the taste buds have gone into overdrive, just like Pavlov's dog.

It does taste exquisite and the three men on the tour with me, Thos Farrell, Mick Walsh and Dishy Walsh, agreed it was the best they ever tasted. Just to prove a point our guide, Ronan, 'forced' us to take a sip of a pint poured straight, without the break and without giving the beer a little time to settle. It wasn't as good. According to Ronan, who has thirty years' experience of working in the brewery, it is all about balance and body, but is it also the intoxicating atmosphere of the Cellar that gives it that extra kick?

Another gem in the brewery is the tasting room, which

is only around fifty years old. Every morning, religiously, the brewers come here to the sound-proofed 'beer basilica' to taste the brew at various stages of production, and of course there is always a placebo thrown in to try and catch out the professionals. What a job!

One of the oldest places in the city is at the centre of our tale: the grey, lonesome-looking, almost forbidding St Francis's Abbey. Built around 1254, it is held captive by a concrete jungle. It once stretched all the way down to the River Nore and the monks living there were completely self-sufficient, with grazing fields, orchards, fruit trees, shrubs and, of course, barley. Ronan explained how the monks were constantly fasting and the beer was, for them, liquid food that kept them going during their all-night devotions. The manufacture of beer at ecclesiastical sites was common across Europe and led, for example, to the astonishingly popular German tradition of beer festivals.

The abbey started as a small rectangular chapel, but then expanded as funds allowed, reaching out from the city walls to the Nore, taking in Evan's Turret, one of the defensive towers that formed an integral part of these walls. Development continued throughout the fourteenth, fifteenth and sixteenth centuries, but expansion was halted by the dissolution of the monasteries in the middle of the sixteenth century, when the Corporation and the Butlers ultimately took control of the land.

Throughout the eighteenth century, the friars moved into parish work but their numbers quickly declined.

By 1766 there were only two friars left in the Kilkenny community, with a couple of other friars working as parish clergy in the diocese. The last friar was Fr Philip Forristal, who worked as a curate in the diocese rather than actually living in a Franciscan community, and the Franciscan connection ended with his death in 1829.

The abbey building was used as a cavalry barracks in the 1700s until the monks came back again, before it was once again put to a civil use, this time as a tennis court. And a Mrs Morrissey who was guardian of the brewery in the late nineteenth century had the floor covered in a green carpet! At present only a few people at a time can visit the abbey, which is under the care of the OPW.

The workers in the brewery built the intimate little oratory next door, during their time off, in the 1950s. It's a place where Mass was said, sometimes to crowds of 150 or 200 people and, as Ronan tells us, 'the very best place in the whole world to say an "Ale Mary"'. It's like a Marian grotto, and a noticeboard on the side wall has memorial cards of brewery workers, one of whom helped to build the place. This little shrine has to be preserved in memory of the men who worked there and of the few who lost their lives here.

Evans Turret, also known as the Castle in the Garden, has remained in private ownership within the St Francis Abbey Brewery compound for generations. In 1650 the Civil Survey described it as 'a little castle in the garden' of the priory. The tower became known as Evans Turret when the land on which it stands was leased by the Corporation to an Alderman Evans in 1724. We know that in 1851 it was still roofed. Located at the extreme north-east corner of the St Francis Abbey Brewery complex, where the Breagagh meets the Nore, it could be accessed by a rising stairway over a vault which collapsed many centuries ago. It has a basement level with an internal arched entrance, a first floor, and an upper level with apertures. Judging from its appearance when still roofed, it is likely that the tower was modified and heightened to form a garden feature overlooking the river in the eighteenth century. The external masonry is in reasonable condition, though there are some external cracks in the tower walls; the internal collapsed stair vault suggests that some movement has occurred in the foundations.

The hope now is that the abbey will finally be given the TLC it requires. A path could link it to the turret, and the concrete around it be removed to allow the soil to breathe again and make it a green oasis. Who knows, in a few years from now Mass might once again be celebrated there by a Franciscan.

Castletown Cox

Castletown Cox is one of the most expensive, beautiful and elegant residences in Ireland. Now home to a real-life lord, it is the former home of a bogus, but much-loved, baron and for many years was the residence of the very popular Charlie Blacque and family. Yet outside of the area around Piltown and Owning, the general public have never heard of it. To appreciate this place, imagine Downton Abbey from the hit ITV series, and you get a sense of how special it is. The gardens are simply breathtaking and the house is pristine. The Irish people owe a great debt of gratitude to the present owner, retired banker and former chairman of the British Conservative Party George Magan, Lord Magan of Castletown, for buying it and for painstakingly restoring it. He is the son of an amazing Irishman born in Athlone, Brigadier Bill Magan, one of the most important figures in Cold War espionage, who served at the very pinnacle of MI5, the British intelligence service. He died in 2012 aged 102, having led an incredible life.

Set amid the rolling hills of South Kilkenny, Castletown Cox is veiled in secrecy, boasting a rich and varied past. It was first built in 1776 for the Protestant Archbishop of

Cashel, Michael Cox, whose family owned it for a number of generations. Architecturally, the house is stunning and is the work of the Sardinian-born canal engineer and architect Daviso de Arcort, who came up with a design which has really stood the test of time. Blessed with a rather large ego and the money to go with it, Cox, who also commissioned the Cashel Palace Hotel in the centre of Cashel as his official residence, wanted something special, and the finished product had the impact he desired. In the grounds, a wonderful house with Italian strains to it also looks exquisite.

Castletown Cox is said to be based on the Villa La Rotunda, a Renaissance villa just outside Vicenza in northern Italy, and on Buckingham House (not palace) in London. Seen for the first time, the sheer scale of the complex symmetry of the entire structure is awesome. The interior is divine, with only the finest materials used in its upkeep, totally in keeping with the original decor, and expert advice sought on all facets of the work.

Built in the Baroque style and three storeys high, the main building has pilasters, huge windows and two U-shaped wings on either side, the ends of each barely touching the main building. At one corner of each of the wings are octagonal slated domes. One of the most eye-catching elements in the design of the house is the use of blue Kilkenny-limestone details set against dressed sandstone on the front and wings. Much of the original plasterwork inside the house was by Waterford's

Patrick Osborne and includes motifs of cherubs, fruit and flowers.

The house has had its fair share of wonderful owners, such as the bogus Baron de Breffny, the son of a London taxi driver turned bookie, who invented a title for himself. The baron and his wife held lavish parties at the house that would last for three days, and people from around Owning, who waited on tables, said that what went on at Castletown Cox would make the excesses of the Celtic Tiger era look like penny-pinching.

The baron's first wife was an Indian princess, but that marriage didn't work out, and he was later married again, to Lady Ulli Sands. On one occasion, a Kilkenny city resident went down to visit the baron on business, and when he walked down from the reception hall there were gentlemen of Oriental extraction standing in morning suits at the door to each of the eight rooms. They were placed there to impress.

Although it now has a new owner, the memory of Brian, Baron de Breffny, and his Rat Pack, still haunts Castletown Cox. He was a tragic figure in the image of F. Scott Fitzgerald's Jay Gatsby, and since his death in 1989 the stories about him abound and have gained embellishment in the re-telling. Here are some that have been verified. He was born in Isleworth, London, in January 1931, to an English-Jewish father, Maurice, and an Anglo-Irish mother (O'Dell). The family had a taxi firm and bookie offices and that's where he earned his first bit of money. He first married Princess Jyotsna Devi, the daughter of His Highness Sir Uday Chand Mahtab, KCIE, Maharajadhiraja Bahadur of Burdwan, India, and although the marriage lasted just long enough to produce a daughter, Sita-Maria, before being dissolved, it was, from the outset, a match largely of convenience. The princess needed a way out of India, Brian needed the money and the standing she brought with her. Unusually, Sita-Maria remained with her father, eventually coming with him to Ireland, where she married Viscount de Vesci of Abbeyleix and had three children.

De Breffny then met his second wife, Ulli. She was the Finnish-born widow of the extremely wealthy Sir Stafford Lofthouse Sands, the former finance minister of the Bahamas and one of the notorious 'Bay Street Boys' – the white businessmen/politicians who controlled the Bahamas at the time. He died in 1972, having become embroiled in a scandal relating to $1.8 million paid to him by the operators of two large local casinos. The money arrived in the guise of consultancy and legal fees, and the payments were hardly unusual by the standards of the Bahamas at the time, but it was nevertheless an embarrassment for Sir Stafford, who left for Italy, where he bought a glorious sixteenth-century, thirty-seven-room villa. The baron was Ulli's fourth and final husband. Those who knew de Breffny never forgot him, and whatever failings he had with his title, he was blessed with a great personality and real charisma.

The people in the townlands of Castletown, Graigue and Ballyhennerbry and across to the village of Owning are extremely protective of the current owner, his guests and their privacy. Lord Magan is, according to locals, kind and easy to deal with and has kept up the tradition of entertaining in the magnificent surroundings of Castletown Cox.

Duiske Abbey

A t the height of its influence, before the dissolution of the monasteries in the sixteenth century, Duiske Abbey, Graignamanagh, was like a mini-Vatican set by the River Barrow. Even today the main building, saved from ruin by the local people, is magnificent, and when you enter through the main door on the north side of the abbey, to the right, a wooden scale model of the monastic settlement in its heyday greets you. The exterior does not prepare you for the beauty of the interior. You can see the ancient stone and high clerestory windows of the nave and there is a real feeling of serenity here. If you want to go to a place that exudes calm, then the abbey and its various little alcoves are the ideal afternoon hideaway. You can almost hear the long-departed monks chanting. When I enter the abbey it always reminds me of a scene from an Inspector Morse mystery; indeed the grounds hide many secrets as they have yet to be properly examined by experts.

But to get to the heart of Duiske Abbey we must think of the generosity of the Normans who gave the land and rents to the abbots, who were more politicians than holy men. This provided not only enormous influence and power, but ownership of some of the best arable land in the country, with salmon and eel weirs, a mill and a complex social structure, with dozens of unvowed monks doing the donkey work while the sixty Cistercians oversaw everything, did the praying and collected the money. Duiske was at the heart of a hugely successful feudal system that did not require any outside help.

To appreciate the original size of the community, you must visualise a main house, chancel, dormitory, individual cells for the hermits and those on special prayer duty for a particularly generous benefactor, an infirmary, lay brothers' domicile, two refectories, reading gallery, abbot's chamber, cellars, kitchen and the abbey building itself, which would have been composed of the nave, north and south transepts and the octagonal tower. Today, there are various little alleyways and streets blocking the abbey's path to the River Barrow, but from the thirteenth to the eighteenth centuries this land was all part of the complex. It had a gatehouse on the river and next to that was the guesthouse.

When you come out of the main entrance, cross the road onto High Street and then continue to St Mullins Street and you reach the abbey's mill. The mill, built by the Cistercians in the thirteenth century, is still used today by Cushendale Woollen Mills. Run by a descendant of Huguenot artisans, it is a flourishing business thanks to the Manaigh Ban, who first diverted the water from the River Duiske, which rises on Brandon Hill.

Left out of the main entrance of the abbey, past the cemetery, is where the beehives, vegetable gardens and pasturelands for the livestock were sited.

Duiske Abbey is similar in style and scale to the Strata Florida Abbey in Cardiganshire, Wales. The church there was consecrated in 1201, a few years before the town of Graignamanagh was founded when the White Monks (so-called because of their undyed woollen habits) arrived in the area. Part of the monks' mission was to look after the poor and needy and they did that for many generations.

William Marshall, who built Kilkenny Castle, was the man responsible for the establishment of the abbey. He was the son-in-law of Strongbow, the leader of the Norman conquest of Ireland. Marshall, the Earl of Pembroke, invited Cistercians from Stanley in England to come to Kilkenny. The monks called the area around Graignamanagh 'The Valley of the Holy Saviour', and spent some months travelling around the Diocese of Ossory before coming to the conclusion that this valley, next to the Barrow, was the best place to build. It was an inspired choice that led to the foundation of the town, the construction of roads, the clearing of marsh and woodland for planting and the bringing of prosperity. A dozen monks started the Cistercian community at Duiske, the minimum allowed under ecclesiastical law, and what the order built, even though it has changed down through the ages, is remarkable.

As late as 1812, the traveller Bernard Trotter was hugely impressed when he visited the ruins of the abbey.

He said: 'I cannot describe how nobly venerable it looked ... nothing could be found venerable and more beautifully interesting in the empire than Graignamanagh [Duiske] abbey.' Matt Doyle, who was from Graignamanagh, once called it the Riviera of the south-east and while this may be a little far-fetched, it certainly had a special place in the heart of internationally acclaimed short-story writer Sean O'Faolain, who penned the definitive biography of Hugh O'Neill. He said of Graignamanagh, where he holidayed on a regular basis, 'the whole valley swoons in an air so delicately moist that it seems too heavy to move, so that on still, wet days even the clouds lie asleep across the distant mountains and one gets the overpowering sensation of steamy growth, of success over nature, of peace as unbroken as the buzzing of the bees.'

The monks at Duiske were very industrious. They managed huge flocks of sheep and had their own woollen mill from where they exported wool to Italy; as early as the thirteenth century they had strong ties with Genoa, one of the great merchant 'Maritime Republics' of the Middle Ages. They also built fish traps on the River Barrow, harvesting salmon and eel.

The abbey hit trouble as early as the late fourteenth century when the Black Death swept through Ireland and Europe. In the first year, the monks cared for the sick who died in the abbey and then the monks themselves fell ill. In 1349 a visitor to the abbey wrote of the impact of the Black Death on the place: 'it is filled with woeful looking men some covered in sores, other spitting up blood. Few recover that have their infection.'

In 1536 the monks were scattered after the dissolution of the monasteries by Henry VIII, and the 9th Earl of Ormonde, James Butler, took over the land. He was a cousin of the last abbot at Duiske, Charles O'Kavanagh, who sold some of the land off to James before the closure, looking after his own welfare. Charles received a pension of £10 a year and possession of nearby Kilkenny Abbey with thirty-eight acres. Some of the other monks went to Regensburg in Germany.

In 1774 the great octagonal tower of the abbey fell down, which was blamed on two goats feeding on the roof. There was a prophecy that the tower would fall the day the devil passed through Graignamanagh. After the collapse an English soldier wrote: 'When we heard the news we shook our heads. That the devil was loose again in Ireland was ill news. It was said that he had not been sighted for certain in our country since the apparition to Saint Moling, near a thousand years before.' Folklore states that the devil appeared to St Moling at a well located a few miles over the border in St Mullins, County Carlow.

Mr John Joyce, in his wonderful work *Graignamanagh – A Town and its People*, said that when the tower crashed to the floor it brought with it the groined roof of the chancel, which had been claimed by Stewart in *Topographica Hibernica* to be 'the finest in the Kingdom'. Mr Joyce said that the ruination was completed a few years later when the marble tree, the central column which supported the vaulted roof of the chapter house, was removed during the night to decorate a County Carlow garden.

Almost 200 years after this 'theft', Graignamanagh's own poet laureate, William O'Leary, wrote the following lines:

A dirge for Duiske, once so great and grand
No white Cistercian in its abbey dwells
Now money loving men possess the land
And house their cattle in its ruined cells.

Later in the dirge he speaks of ghostly monks in the abbey at night and there are many stories of haunted happenings in the chancel and nave; most late at night, after the pubs closed! We learn, for example, from the late Fr Seán Swayne's excellent history of the abbey, that in 1820 Ralf Mordant, later to become leader of the Graignamanagh Band, was in the abbey with his father. He had been holding a candle while his father was decorating the high altar canopy for Christmas. The candle went out and while his father went to find a piece of lighted turf, young Ralf, sitting up on the canopy, heard singing coming from the south transept and passing below him. Ralf was stunned by the grandeur of the melody and said that it was 'all semi-breves'. His father told him it was definitely the monks and that they had been heard many times before.

In 1754 Duiske Abbey was part-renovated by the

Established Church as a place of worship and the local rector had work carried out to fill in the windows, broken, it was alleged, by jackdaws, who had been cracking them with their beaks. However, it was never used and the newly renovated part of the roof was removed in 1805 to be reused at the Church of Ireland in nearby Whitehall.

The graveyard of the abbey is also well worth a visit. What is thought by many to be the finest thirteenth-century effigy of a knight in Ireland lies there, with the figure in armour, cross-legged in the manner of a crusader, armed in transverse-banded mail and seizing a sword. Geraldine Carville, in her book *Norman Splendour*, identifies the knight as Alan Beg, who gave half of the tithes accruing to his huge estate in nearby Ullard in exchange for a burial place there. The churchyard is also home to the Aughtiltan and Ballyogen crosses, dating from the eight and ninth centuries respectively, which were moved to the abbey in the nineteenth century for protection, but these do not receive much attention from anyone.

By the middle of the eighteenth century the abbey was a ruin, and houses had sprung up on all sides using the once proud abbey defences as their back walls. Thus the town of Graignamanagh, which had been fed by the abbey for centuries, devoured what was once the largest enclave of its kind in Ireland.

Rathbeagh – burial place
of King Heremon

The druids still haunt the island of Ireland thousands of years after the coming of Christianity. Echoes of their chants become almost audible as the mist settles on the banks of the River Nore, shortly after it flows from County Laois into Kilkenny and through Rathbeagh, Lisdowney – the fort of the birch trees.

According to Irish mythology, the Milesians ruled Ireland from Kilkenny for centuries and the supposed burial place of their most famous king, Heremon, outside North Kilkenny is almost a secret and certainly a hidden gem of this county's rich and varied heritage. If *National Geographic* were aware of this, they might have a two-hour documentary made, comparing it to the Lost Valley of the Pharaohs in Egypt. The thought is not as far-fetched as you might think – Heremon, the long-lost king of the Milesians, was buried in what is known as the Valley of Death, so called because of the density of hill forts, fairy forts, Iron-Age settlements, Bronze Age communities, Christian relics and medieval ruins around Conahy, Lisdowney, Freshford, Johnstown and Ballyragget. Over a hundred burial sites are spread along the Nore Valley, of which eighty are located between Kilkenny city and Ballyragget alone. On the opposite bank of the river from Rathbeagh, cemeteries are to be found at Ballyconra, Parks Grove, Grange and Lismaine.

That the Milesians did in fact exist outside of the mythology built around them is a fact that has been documented in ancient manuscripts and backed up by recent DNA testing on the bones of the people whose remains are found at the very bottom of these raths, henges and ring forts. Results matched DNA found in Spain, Portugal and North Africa from the same time period, accurately estimated thanks to pollen testing.

In an article in the Lisdowney parish magazine, *The Raven*, in 1990, local historian Tommy Maher concentrates on the link between the Milesians and the mystical, even mythical, Tuatha de Danann (the people of the Goddess Danu, one of the great ancient tribes of Ireland) and the Firbolg (literally 'men in sacks') who ruled Ireland before the de Danann. He writes that the Milesians were followers of Milesius and arrived in Ireland from Spain following a druidical prophecy that they would conquer a western island – their island of destiny (Inisfail). By the time his followers reached Ireland Milesius was dead, but his eight sons were among those who had set sail in thirty ships. When they came ashore, the Tuatha de Danann objected, claiming that the landing would never have succeeded if they had not been taken unawares. A parley was arranged and Amergin, one of the sons of Milesius, proposed that they would withdraw nine waves from the shore and re-attempt a landing. When they did so the Tuatha de Danann used their magic powers to raise a storm which sank some of the ships. Numbered among those lost were five of the sons of Milesius. The landing was successful, however, and the Milesians defeated the Tuatha de Danann at Sliabh Mis in Kerry and at Tailteann in Meath. At this latter battle three of the Tuatha de Danann kings were slain and power passed to the Milesians. The sovereignty of Ireland was now divided between two of the surviving sons of Milesius, Heber and Heremon. Meanwhile, the vanquished Tuatha de Danann retreated into the mounds and raths of Ireland where they have remained ever since. Two years later the two kings quarrelled and a battle was fought in which Heber was defeated and slain, leaving Heremon as the sole ruler of Ireland – the first Ard Rí. Meanwhile Heremon's wife, Tea, died and was buried according to her wishes in Meath. The place of her burial was named Tea-Mur which became Teamhair or Tara. The date given for these events varies, but they happened somewhere between 1600 and 350 BC. The Milesian dynasty reigned for several centuries, until the beginning of the Christian era.

Rathbeagh is actually called Rath Beitheach, the Rath of the Birch Trees, and is situated immediately adjacent to the west bank of the River Nore, three miles south of

Ballyragget in the parish of Lisdowney. It was sited at the meeting of a stream and the Nore to take advantage of a kink in the Nore that allowed for extensive views up and down the river. Today the monument is a large, raised oval earthwork measuring 262 feet across, surrounded by a bank, a deep ditch and a second outer bank. The original entrance was a ramp on the landward side of the earthwork.

It has been suggested by some archaeologists that Rathbeagh is a 'henge' – a place where elaborate ceremonies and gatherings took place in the Neolithic and Bronze Ages. A population explosion appears to have occurred in the prehistoric period throughout the Nore Valley as its thick forests were cleared and field systems such as those recorded by archaeologists at Ballyconra and Foulksrath were laid out to protect crops and livestock, still present today. It seems that Rathbeagh was a village community, but the Nore has washed most of the evidence for this away. No dwellings of these prehistoric farmers have been found in northern Kilkenny, but there has been no full excavation carried out at Rathbeagh. Such work could reveal untold treasures in terms of our past, but until such time as they are investigated we don't know what may be there.

As Cóilín Ó Drisceoil puts it so elegantly, it is the archaeology of death that marks out Rathbeagh and other sites which were used primarily for funeral ceremonies. The body of the very important person was usually cremated and placed in a mound and/or cist which was then surrounded by a circular ditch and bank. Most of the examples found in North Kilkenny have been damaged by ploughing and only their deepest parts – usually the surrounding ditch – remain intact. Called 'ring-ditches', these can only be seen from the air when they appear intermittently as crop marks (they are not, as some have suggested, alien landing sites!).

During Kilkenny County Council's 'Heritage Audit of the River Nore', areas of erosion around the edges of the central platform at Rathbeagh were noted – these produced animal bones and local green-glazed hand-built medieval pottery pieces that suggest the site may have had a late-twelfth to early-thirteenth century phase of occupation. Its defensive siting on the kink in the river implies it was built to control river traffic along the Nore and it could well have been the site of one of the wooden castles first built in North Kilkenny.

In a debate in 2012, the Kilkenny Archaeological Society attempted to put the age-old question – are we Celts? – to rest when it invited four leading authorities to discuss the motion in Kilkenny Castle. While it has always been assumed that we are a Celtic nation, i.e. part of the Indo-European group which in pre-Roman times inhabited Britain, Gaul, Spain and other parts of western and central Europe, modern research has led to differing opinions, with experts from the worlds of archaeology and academia challenging the cosy consensus. Some academics suggest that the Celts' engagement with Ireland was fleeting, unsubstantial and a myth fostered and sustained by political expediency. If this is the case and if our belief that we are descended from the Celts is incorrect then the tantalising question emerges – who are we?

Bishop's Palace

Everything comes down to sex and money – or so the cynics in our society would lead us to believe – so we start our story of the fantastic Bishop's Palace in the oldest part of Kilkenny city with a little summer house built to its side. The 'robing room' next to the palace was never, as far as we know, used for the purpose for which it was intended. Clergy going and coming from the Anglican St Canice's Cathedral to the Bishop's Palace did not use it to change from their altar costumes to their everyday clothes. There is growing speculation that a sophisticated underfloor heating system from the 1700s might have been used to keep female bums warm as they sat in seats in the neo-classical summer house as part of a bishop's harem. The unfortunately named Bishop Pococke would have been able to sneak out of a side door of the palace, down a wooden stairs and across the last few yards without being seen, into what was effectively a sauna, a facility he would have come across during his travels in the Middle East.

Excavations carried out at the robing room in 2011 and 2012, as part of a Kilkenny Archaeology/Heritage Council research programme, show that the eighteenth-century building was constructed over part of St Canice's Monastery – specifically a zone where comb making and metalworking were carried out. Hundreds of pieces of chopped deer antler, the waste from the comb maker's workshop, were found along with pieces of finely decorated 'composite' combs (presumably for removing nits from hair).

The palace itself was saved from dereliction thanks to the decision of the Heritage Council to locate its headquarters there and to the wisdom of the Church of Ireland authorities to sell the house to them to ensure its survival. And when the money is available Ian Doyle, archaeological officer with the Heritage Council, hopes that excavation of the green area directly behind the palace will unearth the exact spot upon which the city of Kilkenny was founded: where St Canice built his church.

It was another pioneer, the appropriately named Bishop Ledred (1317–60), who built the palace. He was extremely puritan and was known to be fond of witch burning, as Dame Alice Kyteler and her maid Petronella found out (to the latter's cost) during a dark period in the history of the city. The construction of the palace started around 1350 and it was built at a high point of the city, overlooking the Nore. It is noteworthy that Ledred used the stones from three churches – St Brigid's, St Nicholas' and St James', located just outside the city wall – in the building of his palace. Colm Murray, architectural officer with the council, has suggested that after the Black Death there were probably very few worshippers around to use these three churches, while Ian Doyle has argued that Ledred (who seems to have been an upstart who started out life as a lowly French friar and not a priest) also wanted to assume control of the entire place. Both point out that it was unusual for a palace to be built so close to a diocesan see (St Canice's Cathedral) and that normally bishops were kept as far away as possible from the actual seat of power because it was felt by hard-working clerics that they were meddlers and more interested in power than in the welfare of the people.

Since its original construction the building has been added to and remodelled over the centuries. Immediately before the Reformation, in the mid-sixteenth century, Bishop Milo Baron (1527–55), had work carried out, including the building of a three-storey tower at the eastern end of the palace. This tower (minus its external staircase) is the most remarkable remaining part of the building and the remains of original window frames can still be seen on its exterior. The tower was constructed as an extension to accommodate male servants, with no access to the female servants on the other side of the wall.

However, in the following century the building's position declined and by 1660 it was described by one observer as being in a ruinous state, without a roof. Things improved in the late seventeenth century when a new roof and new rooms, as well as new windows and doors were added, and this trend continued into the early eighteenth century, when Bishop Charles Este (1735–40) added four rooms and the staircase, which survives today. Archaeological excavations also uncovered the remains of a late seventeenth-/early eighteenth-century kitchen. Today the new pavilion, which is used as a canteen and meeting area, is on the site of this original kitchen, not completely parallel with the palace, to keep true to the original kitchen's footprint.

Ros Willoughby, daughter of the much-loved late Bishop Noel Willoughby, who is buried close to the entrance to St Canice's Cathedral, was the last child to grow up in the palace and walked from there to the cathedral on the day of her wedding, in 1993, to one of the finest Gaelic footballers ever produced by Mayo, Dermot Flanagan. When Katherine Blake of the *Kilkenny People* interviewed Ros she said:

> ... off the butler's pantry, in the place of the Willoughby's kitchen, there is now a lift ... My father would be thrilled to see the lift. He carried all the coal and logs upstairs to the family drawing room and the formal drawing room and we had fires lighting in each every day.

The palace remains a secret, hidden gem of Kilkenny's heritage because of the limestone wall that borders it on one side and the cathedral which dwarfs it on the other. It is located inside the wall on the left-hand side of Vicar Street as you walk towards Troy's Gate (named after a bishop who lived there). Just before the public house are two entrances. The one to the left brings you to the rear and side of the palace. The other, more dignified entrance is from the narrow road directly behind St Canice's Cathedral and beside the Good Shepherd Centre.

The restoration was painstaking and honest. While today's building looks like a Georgian structure, it has hidden depths reaching back to the fourteenth century. Although it is a Heritage Council Office, access is still allowed to the public and it is well worth a visit.

Medieval Towers

$\sim$

This is a tale of two medieval towers, which were an integral part of the once almost impregnable old city walls of Kilkenny. One has been restored with integrity, the other forgotten and in need of attention, even though experts regard it as being of national importance.

By the year 1300, Kilkenny was Ireland's most important inland town, and to defend its inhabitants and their property a stone wall over two metres thick and eight metres high was built around the town. It became the largest walled town in Ireland, with the circuit over two miles long, and enclosed the boroughs of Irishtown and Hightown and the suburb of St John's. Nine lookout towers were incorporated in the wall, of which two survive today.

The first of the surviving two towers is Talbot's Tower, which is once more a proud outpost of the old city. It provides a real focal point for the walls and gives visitors a starting point for their tour of what was once the magnificent defence system of the walled city. It is only when you mount the steps to the top that you can appreciate the scale of that system, incorporating the huge town ditch below, the inner slope of which was provided with a sloping stone wall, a 'base batter' that prevented the enemy from tunnelling beneath the wall. The tower was sited on a low hill and from its parapets there are extensive views in all directions. From its summit, despite the imposition of some horrendous-looking buildings erected over the last fifteen years, you can still see Kilkenny Castle and St Canice's Cathedral and Round Tower, as well as St Mary's Church. It was originally known as St Patrick's Tower in reference to a nearby suburb, while the name Talbot's Tower was an early twentieth-century appellation that alludes to Robert Talbot, a mayor of the city in the fifteenth century who was traditionally credited with building the walls.

For those seeking titillation, we know from excavations carried out during the restoration that the top of the tower has a very spicy history. Finds included fragments of Victorian wine bottles, clay tobacco pipes, hairpins, metal lace chapes (for holding female undergarments in place) and many ladies' buttons. Archaeologist Ben Murtagh has carried out major research work here and has found a dazzling array of artefacts, including .303 bullets and cases which may have been used by Free State forces against the Republicans who occupied Kilkenny Castle during the Civil War in 1922, while a lead musket-shot fired at the tower probably dates from one of the sixteenth-century sieges of the city.

Sadly, the other surviving tower, Evans Turret, is rarely mentioned in terms of the rich mosaic of the heritage of the city, yet it may have been even more important than

Talbot's Tower. We have already met this tower in our tour of the St Francis Abbey Brewery compound. It was known as the Castle in the Garden and the fact that it has remained in private ownership, without public access to it, may have saved it from vandalism or accidental damage. The brewery closes down at the end of 2013 and an archaeological dig at the tower must be a priority, as there is much to investigate, including a collapsed vault, its use as a summer home and its links with the priory which also lies within the confines of what was Smithwick's Brewery. The sale of the brewery to the city means there will be an opportunity to return the polygonal tower to its original beauty.

Evan's Turret is located at the extreme north-east corner of the St Francis Abbey Brewery complex, where the Breagagh meets the Nore, and access is by a rising stairway over the collapsed vault. Getting in can be difficult and involves climbing over the outer wall. It has a basement level, with an internal arched entrance, a first floor and an upper level with apertures. Judging from its appearance when still roofed, it is likely that the tower was modified and heightened in the eighteenth century to form a garden feature overlooking the river.

Over twenty-five years ago, city woman Betty Manning had a dream that what she believed was the last surviving, yet crumbling, tower of the Old City Wall of Kilkenny would be returned to its former glory. At times it seemed a lost cause, especially in 1989 when the stairwell of the structure collapsed. It has since become a testament to what can be done when people come together to work for the benefit of the city. Cllr Paul Cuddihy is the new chair of the City Walls Committee and, knowing him, I'm confident that Evans Turret will soon receive the same treatment as Talbot's Tower.

Swift's Heath

M istresses galore; home of the first patented aeroplane in Ireland; a world-famous satirist loved by Japanese academics; a priceless Prussian of royal extraction – the history of Swift's Heath, one of the most magnificent houses in the south-east, has it all. Located just four miles from Kilkenny city on the road to Ballyragget and dating from the 1640s, this wonderful Palladian, L-shaped building with Corinthian pilasters has direct links with the Shah of Iran, the Tsar of Russia and a host of British aristocracy. It has been at the centre of the Irish and legal world for many different reasons. It not only endures but is in a magnificent condition thanks to the lifelong obsession of a selfless lady who has added even more character to what should be one of the most famous houses in Ireland and yet is a hidden gem.

The most famous resident of Swift's Heath was Dean Jonathan Swift (1667–1745), still regarded as Ireland's greatest satirist and the man who gave us *Gulliver's Travels*. Japanese university professors still call to the house to see where he spent his formative years. Although there have been many biographies, his life at Swift's Heath is shrouded in mystery. His mother abandoned him after his father died and he was raised by his Uncle Godwin, although he had nothing good to say about the man who was *in loco parentis* to him and who ensured he received the best education possible.

The future dean went to Kilkenny College on horseback every day from Swift's Heath and his bedroom has remained largely untouched from the time he stayed there. Entering it you are taken by the views on two sides of the surrounding countryside, but it is the presence of a kneeling chair, owned by the Catholic Bishop of Kildare and Leighlin, Michael Ryan, that catches the eye. It looks so unusual in the childhood bedroom of the former Church of Ireland dean of St Patrick's Cathedral, Dublin.

With six bedrooms, five bathrooms and the oldest indoor toilet in Ireland, Swift's Heath is much smaller than its L shape suggests. It is, however, vast, when you take into account the various barns, outhouses and other buildings still much in use, which are also in superb condition.

The Swift family motto is 'Hasten with caution, by virtue not by blood', or, to twitterise it: 'Be quick without impetuosity'. A dubious example of this philosophy, and by far the most colourful owner of Swift's Heath was Godwin Meade Pratt Swifte, who once owned a palazzo in Venice, which is now the Grand Hotel. Born in 1806, he was what would today be called a bit of a boyo. He was known as Godwin V but called himself Lord Carlingford, a title he plucked from another branch of the family. According to an article in the *Old Kilkenny Review* by his descendant, Geoffrey Marescaux, he took the title to impress his wife-to-be, an Austrian baroness. The article continues: 'He was not faithful, so that husband and wife lived apart – he in Ireland, she in Germany.' Twelve years after marrying the baroness, he 'formed a bigamous union with the daughter of an army officer'. They had three children and when she died she was buried in County Meath as the fictitious Viscountess Carlingford. The children later sued the Swifts, who had been awarded the property at Swift's Heath for their share of the inheritance, but, because they were illegitimate, they did not succeed in recovering the property. Carlingford had argued, while he was alive, that his union to the baroness was illegal in Ireland because she was a Catholic, even though they had entered their civil and religious union on the continent. Little did he think it would come back to haunt his children; some of them anyway. He also had a number of regular female 'callers' to Swift's Heath and maybe this is the reason that many of the Swifts who came after him were so quick to take lovers but slow to get married. After the baroness died he married an Irish woman from an old Tipperary family, who gave him a legitimate heir.

Godwin V or Lord Carlingford had a huge interest in aeronautics and designed and patented the first aeroplane in Ireland. He built the plane in the dining room of Swift's Heath, but realised when it was finished that it would not fit through the door. When knocking the door out didn't work, he had part of the wall demolished to remove the plane intact. He then had the contraption hoisted on top of Foulksrath Castle, which he owned at that time, and had it attached to a catapult-like structure. He was to have been the pilot, but instead convinced his butler to get into the contraption. As he was helped into the seat, the servant is said to have uttered: 'Ours is not to question why.' Of course, the plane nose-dived and the butler was left with a number of broken bones. It is claimed by Mr Marescaux in the *Old Kilkenny Review* that the poor man received Danville House, just outside Kilkenny city, for his troubles. The plane is described as 'an aerial chariot or apparatus for navigating the airs' in documents kept by the late George Swifte Ewbank Briggs, who moved to Coolbawn House, Castlecomer, having sold Swift's Heath.[11] Some years ago an engineer with Boeing visited Swift's Heath and saw the plans for the chariot – she said that with a few tweaks it would have flown. So he wasn't that mad after all.

Foulksrath Castle was part of Swift's Heath until the 1940s, when it was sold to An Óige as a youth hostel due to the intervention of one of the country's finest writers, Hubert Butler from Bennettsbridge. It changed hands for £200. Sadly, it is now closed and is beginning to deteriorate.

---

11 It's unclear why he chose to use Swifte Briggs rather than Briggs Swifte.

The innovative Godwin also brought running water into Swift's Heath at a time when no other home in Ireland had it and introduced the first inside toilet in the country. He diverted a stream towards the house, and each morning two men would pump hundreds of gallons of water into tanks on a flat roof. The current owner had to have these removed for safety reasons. Lord Carlingford made Swift's Heath, in some ways, self-sufficient, with huge vegetable gardens, an orchard, tillage fields, cattle and dairy cows, as well as horses.

Major Earnest Godwin Meade Briggs Swifte is another fascinating person who lived in and owned Swift's Heath. He ended up an honorary general in the Persian Army and when a Persian prince, Ishmael, visited Ireland in 1920s he stayed at Swift's Heath. He was also a friend of the last Tsar of Russia and visited him shortly before the 1917 Revolution. In a photograph that survives of a secret meeting between the Tsar and the Shah of Iran, Major Briggs Swifte can also be seen with his back to the camera.

There was a certain chivalrous side to the Swifte men and this was highlighted when Major Briggs Swifte was serving with the British Army in the First World War. He was moving across wasteland in the aftermath of a battle when he came across a fatally wounded German officer. The major spoke fluent German and the dying man asked him to remove his personal papers from his pocket and give them to his family. The major went to Germany after the war, where he found the officer's two daughters. One of them, Fräulein Ella Von Kleinshmidt, returned with him to Ireland and became his mistress at Swift's Heath, while the other daughter became the first female head of police in the German city of Bonn.

The couple kept pet pigs, and each morning in his old age Major Briggs Swifte was pushed out in his wheelchair to greet them and give them their breakfast by hand. They would then be allowed to roam around the estate and, at the end of the day, the major would sound a hunting horn and they would return for their dinner before being locked up for the night. According to local people, they were better fed than the servants, and dined on such delicacies as peanuts. Ella captivated all who met her. After Major Briggs Swifte died she married an elderly farmer living close by in Talbotsinch.

The last Swifte to reside at Swift's Heath was George Swifte Ewbank Briggs. He took possession in 1957, having served in the British Army in the Second World War and then spent twelve years in India. In 1971 he sold the place to the Lennons. Brigitte Lennon (née Dorpmund), from outside Hanover, has been a fabulous owner of Swift's Heath and her hospitality is legendary. I am indebted to her for keeping the memory of the Swifts alive and for the upkeep of the old house. Remarkably, she is the first non-Swift to have lived in the house for over 300 years.

Tybroughney

When the Vikings, the Danish branch, swept up the River Suir, their tidal march was stopped at Tybroughney and it was here they settled and subsequently perished. It is said that the cries of hundreds of Norsemen, their wives and children, killed during a massacre in the tenth century by a Munster clan, can still be heard at night in the rooms of Tybroughney Castle. Were these the screams heard by Robert Dowley (now secretary of the Iverk Agricultural Show) as a child, or were they the sound of poachers being caught taking salmon from the River Suir, a few hundred yards away?

The Vikings were not the first settlers at Tybroughney. There has been a human presence there since long before the arrival of Christianity. Early finds in the area include axe heads along the river dating back 8,000 years. After the massacre in AD 980 the Danes re-established the settlement, although that was not the end of the violence recorded in the area. In 1462 what became known as the Battle of Piltown was also fought there, the only battle fought on Irish soil as part of the War of the Roses. It involved a major confrontation between the local Ormonde lords and the Fitzgeralds, with Thomas Fitzgerald leading the victorious side for the House of York. Almost 10,000 men fought, and the losing side recorded the deaths of 400 horsemen alone.

Canon Carrigan in his *History and Antiquities of Ossory*, Vol. 4 (Dublin 1905), says that there was at Tybroughney in ancient times, 'a town well inhabited and in high repute, particularly on the arrival of the English'. According to local historian Mary O'Shea, the 'English' referred to here are the Anglo-Normans. In common with many early Christian foundations, Tybroughney grew and developed around a monastery. This monastic settlement expanded and eventually incorporated the parish church, graveyard, monastery, monks' huts, forge and micro-brewery, and perhaps also a mill and farmland. The rath at Tybroughney, Fiddown and lookout posts on nearby hills are typical of the 1200s in Kilkenny and indicate a complex defence system built to defend the surrounding lands.

The present castle on the site dates from the fifteenth century. It stands on the remains of an earlier stone castle built to replace a wooden castle on the site in 1185, on the orders of Prince John when he passed by, having sailed upstream from Waterford city. This wonderfully robust fortification, with walls nine feet thick, is at the heart of a microclimate found nowhere else in Ireland: the alluvial soil linked with the sheltered lower valley of the Suir gives a unique protection from the elements and ensures that it is almost always one or two degrees warmer than places even a few miles away on the far side of the South Kilkenny 'mountains'.

In the last 2,000 years the water levels of the tidal Suir have increased by six feet. Even in 1185, boats had to anchor downstream at Grannagh Castle at low tide, and set out again when the tide came in to get to Tybroughney. It must be wondered whether water levels will go up another six feet in the next two millennia.

The throw-away line 'Not everyone can live in Tybroughney' has been used for hundreds of years when local people talk about the microclimate by the Suir, where orchards abound and where milk yields are well above the national average, where much of the country's vegetables are grown and where yields of grain are on average 10 to 15 per cent above the national average per acre. It is now home to the O'Shea's Iverk Produce, one of the largest and most respected fruit and vegetable producers in these islands.

A survey of the area around Tybroughney throws up more questions about its history than answers. Is there a Norse longboat at the bottom of the Suir at Tybroughney? Was Tybroughney a stop-off point for Roman refugees? The uniquely Roman symbols in Tybroughney cemetery certainly suggest this. Robert Duggan says:

[I] believe [they] may have come to Ireland after the fall of the Roman empire as slaves and clerics. The final stand and last remnant of Roman rule was in west Wales. St Patrick was not our only import, and the transition from Bronze Age to an island of saints and scholars was a little too sudden to have been without import. Were we a lifeboat for the scholars of the western Roman empire? In Kilkenny there are a few sites with real and accumulating evidence of this.

The Tybroughney stone which is on Dowley's farm and just to the east of the castle is dominated by centaurs and Roman symbols, which links in to Roman remains found in such places as Freestone Hill. Robert Duggan also tells us that an early Christian monastery was established at Tybroughney by St Madomnec, who studied in St David's, Wales, and that he may have imported the Scottish and Roman symbols from post-Roman Britain. Madomnec also set up a church in Balbriggan in Dublin and was Bishop of Ossory, but he retreated to become a hermit in his final days. He is reputed to have brought the first domesticated bees to Ireland.

Tybroughney is a blessed place, and at its heart, surveying it all, is Tybroughney Castle (which literally translates as the well of St Fachtna, who was Bishop of Lismore for a time). The castle stands proudly on the corner of Leinster and at one point in its illustrious past was guardian of the border between Munster and Leinster. The Mountgarret family lived here before being displaced by the forces of Oliver Cromwell, when it was given to Sir Algernon May. Robert Duggan describes better than anyone else the history of the castle:

Fished, farmed and forded for eight thousand years; invaded

on the tide for conquest and culture; domesticated by Celtic monks bringing Roman symbols; haunted by fallen Danes and Normans; a king-built castle to face the men of Munster; battleground of Roses, corn and Fenians and bypassed by rail, motor-way and Celtic tiger.

Standing on the restored ramparts on top of Tybroughney Castle, the visitor can enjoy amazing views of Waterford, Tipperary and Kilkenny – the castle dominates the breathtaking scene and looking out from here you can see why it was so important as a boundary between the two provinces. You can just make out the pattern of the settlement that surrounded it – the plan of the church (of which one ivy-covered wall remains), the churchyard, the mill and the forge that made it a village long-since removed from human memory. You can also see the imprint of the deep channel, now completely covered over, which allowed boats to go from the castle to the Suir and where the first cot net fishermen worked the river, catching salmon and trout. On my visit there with local historian Robert Duggan, we knocked on the front door to find Louis Dowley standing on a chair putting up a rather delicious metal candleholder. I received a warm South Kilkenny welcome from him and his wife, Daphne, the current custodians, and was given the freedom to roam the castle.

As we left the main reception room, below us was the new oak floor which looks majestic. Above us, the twenty-five-foot-long timber beams rescued from a decaying mill form the base for the floorboards holding up the first floor. To the side is the old farmhouse dating back hundreds of years; it is similar in design to the one attached to Clomantagh Castle, but not as ornate. As at Clomantagh, we suspect that walls from various outer defences at Tybroughney were used to build the house and the large number of farm buildings which surround this working dairy farm.

This former Ormonde stronghold has received a new lease of life from the Dowley family and the tricolour waves proudly from its ramparts. It is one of only a handful of castles that has survived in Kilkenny and, thankfully, a family steeped in the history of South Kilkenny decided to restore Tybroughney. The castle restoration is a long-term project and recent renderings with the correct lime plaster have gone a long way to making the castle dry and habitable. Louis Dowley has also done a magnificent job of cladding the roof. The Dowleys continue to do an admirable job of keeping this irreplaceable part of Kilkenny history safe.

Ballybur Castle

B allybur Castle is captivating. Although relatively small, it has been completely refurbished using original materials. Its fortunes fluctuated with those of one of Kilkenny's oldest families, the Comerfords. This most secret of hidden gems has been saved from ruin by a canny Scot, Frank Gray, with a love of heritage and Kilkenny. He has painstakingly restored this important landmark, built in the reign of Queen Elizabeth I, and returned it to its former glory.

Located a few miles out of Kilkenny city on the Callan Road, on a left-hand turn at Cuffesgrange, the castle is just far enough off the main road to go unnoticed by most. It is five storeys high with a sentry lookout, a keep, a murder hole, a priest's room and all the important features of a Tudor castle. But it has an authenticity that is unparalleled in Ireland and unlike Kilkenny Castle, which is a mish-mash of various periods, Ballybur is a plain, dignified, yet exquisite castle dating from 1588. It was from here that the leader of one of Kilkenny's most prominent families was sent to Connaught during the Cromwellian conquest. The Comerfords suffered for their Catholicism and their lack of guile, along with the Duke of Ormonde (Butler), who was related to them. Unlike Butler, however, they never found their way back into favour with the king. They became the quintessential Wild Geese and although other prominent Catholic families from Kilkenny managed to return from Connaught, the Comerford family of Ballybur never did. They seemed to pay a heavier price than most for their involvement in the failed Jacobite rebellion and in the decades after leaving their estates, which measured thousands of acres, they often did not have enough to eat. The fact that Archbishop Rinuccini stayed at Ballybur Castle in 1645 on his way to Kilkenny for the hugely important Confederation of Kilkenny may have militated against them when Cromwell arrived to put down the rebellion.

The Gray family has carried out magnificent work, but they are only the latest keepers of the flame of Ballybur. Frank bought it from the Marnell family in 1979 and the last three people to live there, Margaret, Tommy and Eileen Marnell, are remembered fondly in the locality. The last owner before the Grays was Nicholas Marnell, who died eleven years ago. He is also believed to have been the last person to be born in the castle, although he hadn't lived there since he was a child.

The allure of Ballybur is encapsulated in a stained-glass window located at the very top of the castle in the main room, under the roof, depicting what looks like Adam in the Garden of Eden. The grey figure in a blue background with an orange sky is visible from the courtyard below.

The piece stands as a testament to Nicholas Marnell and his promise that he would hand Ballybur over to someone who would show it the love it needed to shine again. Commissioned by the Grays, the window is the work of artist Shane Grincell, Nicholas Marnell's grandson. What a connection and what a piece of art, which would do justice to anything that the late Harry Clarke produced.

However, it is the Comerford link that makes Ballybur famous – the time when Kilkenny was considered the capital of Ireland and the papal nuncio, Archbishop Giovanni Battista Rinuccini, stayed there on his way to Kilkenny for the Confederation in the city on 12 November 1645. A rosary presented to John Comerford by Rinuccini is kept in Rothe House and was presented to the Kilkenny Archaeological Society by a descendant of John Comerford, Fr Langton-Comerford, who was based in America.

When Cromwell came and de-roofed the castle, he sent the Comerfords to Connaught and the castle and its 390-plus acres were given to a Bryan Mansergh, a direct ancestor of the former Fianna Fáil junior minister and advisor to Charlie Haughey, Dr Martin Mansergh, who has visited the castle on a number of occasions. The castle passed from the Manserghs to the Deigans to the Marnells. Frank Gray's son, Ruan, tells us that there is little known about the period between 1655 and 1841, when the Deigan family, including Thomas Deigan, were the occupiers of Ballybur. The Marnell sisters married into the Deigan family and their Marnell relatives occupied Ballybur until Frank and his wife Aifric bought it in 1979.

Theirs is a story of a young man from Dunfermline in Scotland (which is very similar in terms of heritage to Kilkenny) and his wife coming to Kilkenny to start a new life in 1978 and seeing the advertisement in Seamus Callanan's window on High Street, Kilkenny, of a castle for sale. Their arrival in Kilkenny was not an accident. Aifric is a daughter of the great Irish scholar Colm O'Lochlainn, a Volunteer in the 1916 Rising, who was from Kilkenny, so for her it was a kind of homecoming. There was no roof back then and one of the first jobs the couple worked on was the parapet, ensuring that the remaining masonry didn't fall.

Everyone thought Frank Gray was mad to pay £20,000 for what he was told was essentially a load of stones. But as well as being a civil engineer, Frank had another skill. He was gifted with stone and had always yearned to be a full-time stonemason, but circumstances did not allow it. So he has worked with Kilkenny Corporation and Kilkenny County Council for the last thirty-four years, but also spent his spare time working on the castle, first the interior and later the exterior. He was lucky in some respects, although you wouldn't think so to look at what he originally purchased. After the removal of the roof, by Cromwell we are told, the castle was capped at an angle to allow the water to run off through a gulley, ensuring that it was essentially sealed and that the four remaining storeys underneath were dry. The other thing that helped was the bricking up of the windows. Oddly, Frank has never slept a night in the castle, saying that he had no real mind to do so because of all the early mornings he spent in it working on the interior. He stays in the little house right next to it.

He did most of the work himself and only enlisted the help of experts when needed. He and Aifric were constantly sourcing materials and storing them. There were only two outside contracts for the entire work on the castle, both carried out by the Cantwells – Ignatius, Mark and Pat – and Frank is delighted with the quality of the work produced by this Kilkenny family.

The ground floor was originally used to store goods, people and livestock in times of danger. Now it has a fully fitted kitchen. Going through the back door, you enter a secluded south-facing patio area with a large fireplace. The first floor consists of an immense bedroom with a four-poster bed and niches in the walls for sleeping. There are also a smaller double room and a very elegant bathroom, containing the largest Victorian bath I've ever seen.

On the second floor you enter a substantial room with more deep niches in the walls for sleeping. During the daytime hanging tapestries covered these niches and the room was used as a living space. Now this floor is a huge double-height dining room, complete with chandelier, and close by there is also a small kitchen to prepare light meals. It has a medieval stone fireplace and a long dining table with church pews, seating up to twelve people. Off this room is a comfortable bedroom containing two beds and windows overlooking the castle grounds, as well as a very elegant shower room with a toilet, shower and hand basin.

The third floor, with its vaulted ceiling, which was once the family chapel, is now another bedroom. This floor also has a shower room with toilet and sink. From a little hallway you can peep through a narrow doorway onto the dining room below. The fourth and top floor, once the state apartment, is now a magnificent baronial-style drawing room, with an oak-beamed ceiling (left exposed), a stone fireplace and a giant chandelier. There are several lounge seats, a table and chairs, plus a beautifully hand-crafted swing in one of the alcoves. Heavy curtains make the room very cosy in the evenings. The four windows, each facing the cardinal points, offer magnificent views. There is also a secret room, once used as a priests' hole or to keep prisoners. Stairs lead up to the ramparts, where on a fine day you can see Mount Leinster and Slievenamon.

Ballybur is bewitching and the cantilever stair made for right-handed people to defend the castle from intruders coming up is wonderful. The Grays have been totally true to this hidden gem, using original materials in the restoration, and this has involved a lot of work. For instance the oak used was bought from Coillte in the late 1970s and kept in Kilmoganny until twenty years later when Frank had it cut by Brett's of the Sion Road. For some of the floors he used black Kilkenny marble produced by Feely Stone in

Kellymount, Goresbridge, where those Comerfords who were not banished to Connaught by Cromwell ended up. Aifric and Frank have spent years finding suitable pieces for the rooms and the hunt continues.

A castle like this is never completely finished and there are always jobs to do. It has to be whitewashed every eighteen months and there is the odd drop of rain still getting in. Frank, who is known for his placid nature, said he never worried that he would not complete the job and he is dogged when he starts a project – he will finish it or die in the attempt. I am glad he is able to share his love of the place with so many visitors who rent it out, which helps to pay for the ongoing upkeep of this glorious Tudor castle.

St Mary's Church and Graveyard

~~~~~

S ome graves in modern cemeteries are regarded by many to be a little over the top, although decorated with the best of intentions. But if you want to see real burial bling then go and visit St Mary's Church (not to be confused with St Mary's Cathedral) and burial ground off High Street, in St Mary's Lane, Kilkenny. In many cases, the Machiavellian medieval merchant princes of the city paid for these memorials to be erected in their honour before they died. For example, John Rothe's magnificent tomb, for himself and his wife Mary Archer, was completed seven years before his death. To put in perspective the amount of funds that were lavished on these grave markers, you could have bought a good-sized farm in the sixteenth or seventeenth century for the cost of the decorated monuments erected by wealthy families during that period. These memorials have stood the test of time and provide us with a hugely valuable insight into the lives of the families who ruled the city when it was regarded as the centre of power in Ireland.

The sixteenth and seventeenth centuries were really the golden period of Kilkenny city. The merchant princes who owned the city centre and controlled every facet of life in it left us with the imprint for the new modern city, and its medieval fabric makes it one of the nicest in the islands off the coast of Europe. St Mary's was at the centre of this world. The church is not, on first inspection, particularly impressive visually, especially since a major part of it was knocked down a few centuries ago. However, it is one of the most important historical and heritage sites in Ireland and has what is regarded as the best collection of medieval/Renaissance tomb slabs in the country. St Mary's also reflects the fortunes of various monarchs and their religious leanings over the centuries. For hundreds of years ownership see-sawed between the Protestants and Catholics, until it was finally deconsecrated in 1951.

The church was built in the late twelfth century as a chapel for the then newly constructed Kilkenny Castle. It was chosen for its central location within the walled town (not yet a city), and Cóilín Ó Drisceoil explained to me that even today it is the first thing you see when you look from the windows of Kilkenny Castle which overlook the Rose Garden. As it was used for civil as well as religious events, such as corporation meetings, the town council gave the church and graveyard financial support, and an annual four pence was collected from each hall and a half penny from each stall or shop to fund its upkeep.

During renovations to the church in the 1960s the monument room was created and incorporated into the

north transept of the church. It houses a fine thirteenth-
century Gothic fluted font and a number of memorials to
the Garvey, Watson, Archer, Murphy, Dunphy and Rothe
families. It also contains a number of inscribed medieval
tombstones and a stone which marked the entrance to a
crypt that lies sealed beneath its floor. The contents of this
room are linked closely to the stone screen to the right of
the entrance door where six heraldic shields of some of the
old families who are represented in the monument room
(Pembrokes, Shees, Rothes, Kellys, Archers, Daniels)
were placed for safety many years ago. Made of Kilkenny
limestone with a raised surrounding frame, they measure
roughly two feet by three feet and were originally used
by the old merchant families to adorn and mark out their
homes at Hightown, now High Street.

In this room there is also a marble plaque to the
Kingsmill family, all born in Kilkenny, and one entry in
particular caught my attention: 'William born 1753, an
officer of the 66th Regiment who served through the
Peninsular Wars and St Helena, guarding Napoleon and
later Lt Col in the Canadian Militia, served for 21 years
as sheriff of Niagara.' What a life. The families who paid
for the monuments still own them and I wonder what
would happen if they wanted to remove them!

To the west of the church is the handsome tomb of
William and Margareta Goer from 1351. We learn
from Katherine Lanigan and Gerald Tyler's publication
Kilkenny: it's architecture and history (Belfast, 1987) that

it provides visitors with an image of the kind of costume worn by the burgesses of Kilkenny in the second half of the fourteenth century, and John Bradley tells us in *Discover Kilkenny*:

> The patronage and upkeep of St Mary's was a visible sign of the pride and wealth of the burgesses, its tombs and chapels reflected their status and it was an important venue for civic ritual. Both church and bell tower, which was evidently spacious, were frequently used for meetings of the corporation and of the town court … In the sixteenth century, if not before, it was one of the principal locations for the performance of the town plays.

Also noteworthy is the tomb of Sir Richard Shee, a three-storey edifice with the twelve apostles around the base and a superstructure which, according to Lanigan and Tyler, depicts Faith, Hope and Charity.

In the early 1960s a decision was made to transform the church building into a parish hall in order to secure the site. The Freemasons, who have been part of Kilkenny life for generations, decided to sell their old premises and incorporate their new meeting rooms into this building. For the last forty-seven years, the 'Brethren' have been located on the first floor of St Mary's and the funds raised from the sale of their old premises greatly assisted in the refurbishment. Lodge No. 642 is a beautiful chamber, full of colourful banners and insignia, yet few have been allowed to see it. The Kilkenny Lodge is part of the Provincial Grand Lodge of south-eastern counties.

Local people have their own memories of St Mary's: the once-a-month Church of Ireland dances; games of badminton; 'meals on wheels' lunches; paintings hanging there during Arts Week; and all kinds of meetings. Thankfully vandalism of the site has stopped (at one point tomb slabs were thrown over John's Bridge) although the damage that was done will take a lot of time and money to correct. But St Mary's now stands on the verge of a new era of greatness thanks to Kilkenny Borough Council and other partners who want to transform it. The council purchased the church and graveyard from the Church of Ireland in 2009, with financial support from the Department of Environment, Heritage and Local Government and the Heritage Council. The site is now entering a new phase in its history, when it is hoped that it will once again become a vibrant part of city life. The vision is to renovate and restore the church, turning it into a museum of national significance and incorporating an archive containing notable local artefacts there. That would mean that important pieces of Kilkenny's history, in storage for many years in Dublin and elsewhere, would be returned to the city once more.

The restoration of St Mary's is important for the people of Kilkenny as it will increase appreciation of the lives of those in the sixteenth, seventeenth, eighteenth, nineteenth and twentieth centuries. It will also shed light on those who really founded modern Kilkenny, such as the Shees, Rothes and others. What looks like a drab old church is indeed one of the most priceless gems in the city's arsenal of heritage places.

Brandon Hill

The purest and best tasting water in Kilkenny (which is free), a double shooting still recalled and the spirit of the country's most notorious highwayman are only part of why Brandon Hill (named after St Brendan the Navigator) occupies such a deep-rooted place in the psyche of the people of Kilkenny, especially those of Graignamanagh. Most people living around Graignamanagh will tell you they have only ever been to the summit once, and many have never been. Yet stories about it seem to dominate the town and it is as if the people of Graignamanagh are living in the shadow of the hill, topped by a giant cairn and other Neolithic features. These make Brandon Hill the most spectacular place in the county as well as being the highest point (1690 feet) above sea level.

It should be compulsory for everyone who lives in or visits Kilkenny, who is able, to walk to the summit of Brandon and take in the commanding views on all sides. There is a direction indicator on top that points out all the main geographical features around you: you can see the Saltee Islands and every mountain range in the east of the country, as well as the winding route of the River Barrow as it meanders down towards St Mullins and on to New Ross.

However, there is one haunting picture from the past that is hard to escape when it comes to Brandon and for this I am indebted to John Joyce and his beautiful book, *Graignamanagh – a Town and its People.* On the lowest edge of poverty were women whose only source of income was the heather that they cut from the side of the hill and then carried down to sell in the town and on the quay, which was used for animal bedding. This practice was carried out from before the time of the famine, right up to the turn of the twentieth century. These Bresna women are gone, but not forgotten. A poem given to me by Billy Hoare encapsulates their hard life and it is important that the present generation understand them and what it means to really struggle in life. The author of the poem was the late Kate O'Leary from Lower Main Street, Graignamanagh, and these lines were first printed in 1901:

A Bresna pulled from Brandon
Here at your mercy lies,
I pray you look upon it
With a kindly critic's eyes,
For sake of hill and valley,
And pleasant days at home
Give fáilte to the bucket
Wherever it may roam.

Over the course of centuries, Brandon Hill has been attracting people. Thousands of years before the coming of

Christianity and the erection of a wooden cross complete with electric lights, fires blazed on the hill that could be seen for hundreds of miles on a clear night. The druids, worshipping a selection of deities, were central to this place: where better to gaze at the stars and the moon with which our ancestors had such a huge affinity? There is a giant cairn at the very top of Brandon and a number of Neolithic sites have been found on the hillside, including an enclosed area believed by archaeologists to have been used for rituals and some kind of sacrifice, animal or maybe even human. There are also two Norman moated sites on the side of the hill and these are believed to have been used by the monks of Duiske Abbey as sites for prayer in the summer months.

The hill has seen its share of sadness and heartbreak. The Great Hunger of 1845 had a severe impact on the Sallybog families who lived for generations, up to the 1840s, on the north-western slope of Brandon, semi-protected from the prevailing wind. The potato blight wiped out a whole village, a community of mountain people.

On 6 August 1888 a young poacher and a gamekeeper were shot on the slopes of the hill, an event that is still discussed in detail around Graignamanagh. John Joyce gives an excellent account of the death of the two men, and E. M. Hughes writing in the *Old Kilkenny Review* of 1994 provides even more detail. The story begins with three men – Pierce Dreelin of Ballycrinnigan, Patrick

Byrne of Ballybeg, St Mullins, and James Doran of Knockmanus, Borris – staying overnight in what is now Murphy's pub, The Rower, before crossing the Barrow and heading on to Brandon Hill to hunt illegally with three trained gun dogs. At the time, Hughes explains, Brandon was divided, half owned by Lord Clifden of Gowran and the other half belonging to the Tighe estate at Inistioge. A small stream separated the land and the three men strayed over this boundary into the Clifden preserve. Having bagged a number of birds, they then returned to the Tighe land. Three gamekeepers working for Clifden followed them onto the Tighe land and after words were spoken one gamekeeper, Michael Walsh, fired a single shot and killed Patrick Byrne's dog. Hearing the dog squeal, Byrne returned and shot Walsh. Byrne himself was then fatally wounded in the thigh and he died on the hillside.

At the inquest into Byrne's death, it was found that Michael Walsh was guilty of manslaughter because he had shot Byrne on Tighe land and not Clifden land. A warrant for his arrest was issued but the gamekeeper died a few hours later.

Hughes reports at the end of her enthralling and incisive article that she attended an event on 7 August 1988 at Brandon Hill where a commemorative plaque to both poacher and gamekeeper was unveiled, with a large crowd from St Mullins, The Rower, Inistioge and Graignamanagh present. The inscription reads: '1888–1988 to commemorate the tragic death of Patrick Byrne of Ballybeg and Michael Walsh of Inistioge resulting from a shooting incident in this area on August 7 1888.'

To get to Brandon Hill you turn off the Graignamanagh bypass and take the turn where the statue of the monk now stands. Keep driving until you come to the metal barrier. Here there is room for a few cars on the town side of a locked gate and it is only a short walk up to Freney's Well. This is named after the highwayman known as Freney the Robber, who was said to have buried some of his loot in a rabbit burrow on the hill while being pursued by soldiers and then, on returning, was unable to find it. Who knows, it could still be there! Michael Holden in his book, *Freney the Robber – The Noblest Highway Man in Ireland*, gives a wonderful account of his dramatic life. Freney was supposed to have been very chivalrous with the ladies in the coaches he robbed or held for ransom. But when he was caught and sentenced to death, he got off due to the influence of the Earl of Carrick, who, it is said, owed Freney a favour that had something to do with a woman. However, part of the deal was that Freney would give up eight of his gang and they were hanged. Freney actually published his memoirs in 1750 and died an old man of natural causes.

Local people have inserted a black pipe at Freney's Well to access the *aqua pura* which has been filtered through the heather. Little benches have been made and on a good day you can sit there and look at the view of Coppenagh and Mount Leinster. 'On the warmest day of the year, the water from the bowels of Brandon would shatter your teeth,' Billy Hoare, showband member, former postman and local historian, claims. The water tastes delicious, with no tang of fluoride. It's a wonder no one ever thought of bottling it. With a bit of branding and marketing it could be a huge hit – 'The Robber Freney's Water'.

Having relaxed there, if you feel up to it, you can walk to the top – there is a looped walk or a more direct route, there isn't much difference. I suggest you go up one way and come down the other. As you climb to different levels you can understand why so many people have been drawn to the place. The top is like a mini plateau and it's impossible to see the terrain below unless you are on the western ledge coming towards the River Barrow.

More could be done to promote Brandon Hill, with exact directional signs and a large map showing all the main features of the hill, which is made up mainly of granite but with deposits of marble and iron. This hill has a long and fascinating history that deserves to be available to all those who visit it.

Tudor Kilkenny

B y far the most important period in the life of Kilkenny was the Tudor era, culminating in the Confederation of Kilkenny when the mighty and good of the country descended on the city for a national parliament which first sat in October 1642. Part of the reason Kilkenny was chosen was its affluence, with mansions, huge gardens, orchards and the millionaire lifestyle lived by its more wealthy inhabitants. Merchants such as the Shees, Langtons and Rothes built incredibly lavish homes and brought in a set of planning rules to control the corporation. They created a fabulous streetscape which is full of character and is the envy of many other towns and cities across Ireland and Europe.

The Tudor era was in effect the golden era of the city, the Renaissance period of Kilkenny's rich history. There are glimpses of Tudor architecture everywhere if you know where to look, for example the 500-year-old archway into Seamus Callanan's auctioneering business on High Street. The huge fireplace dating from 1610 that is part of Elvery's sports shop on High Street is worth investigating too, as above it is the Shee family armorial plaque that bears the initials ES, referring to Elias Shee who owned the house in the seventeenth century.

There are also the remains of a derelict Tudor building, hidden from view and in desperate need of care. If you go up William Street in the city centre and take the first left in through the large gates, you will see it, or what is left of it, straight in front of you. It once faced the Tholsel (City Hall) and St Mary's Church, situated in what was a posh area to live in back then. On the side of this forlorn, yet captivating, shell of a building there is a 'Fógra' asking the public to aid the Commissioners of Public Works in preserving it. It is in stark contrast to the building next to it, The Hole in the Wall, which has been painstakingly restored by heart specialist Michael Conway. Another gem from the reign of Queen Elizabeth I, this is the inner house of a complex built in 1582 by Martin Archer, a member of one of the ten great merchant families of the city. The Archers lost everything in 1654 after Kilkenny fell to the Cromwellians. The Archer property eventually became part of the Duke of Ormonde's estate. In the late seventeenth century a hole was punctured in the wall to gain access from High Street, hence the name The Hole in the Wall. By the late 1700s the venue was a supper-house of renown or ill repute, depending on which records you choose to believe. It was frequented most nights by the Earl of Ormonde and his guests, personalities such as Henry Grattan and Sir Jonah Barrington. It was also a favoured haunt of Captain Arthur Wellesley, who was stationed at Kilkenny barracks before being seconded to the British Army in Spain and India, and eventually becoming Duke of Wellington and later British prime minister. The house developed a name for unruly behaviour and sexual misadventures which led to its closure.

Thanks to Michael Conway it has recaptured its magic and is an excellent music venue. He started the conservation-restoration work in 1999 and while it is still a work in progress it is now a fantastic venue for all kinds of shows in intimate surroundings. The house is again roofed, with cut-stone hooded Elizabethan mullioned windows, original flagstones, hexagonal chimney and oak doors. The inside consists of an upper floor and small gallery which comprised the living apartment of the Archer family. It has been restored and fitted out with a sixteenth-century oak floor and furniture sourced both locally and in Oxford, where Dr Conway spent a good deal of his professional life. The main room measures approximately twenty by twenty feet. The ground floor has become a rustic tavern made from oak beams from the 1582 structure, floor boards and other original oaks.

Besides The Hole in the Wall there are many other properties on High Street and Parliament Street that boast modern façades, but to the rear you can see the original Tudor design and workmanship. The hidden world of secret passageways (one linking most of High Street) gives glimpses of former grandeur, 500-year-old arches, window frames and wooden beams. Many of the lovely houses, such as Martin Crotty's residence on Lower Patrick Street, have Georgian façades but they are actually

Tudor in origin, and the people who live in these homes have retained the Tudor elements even though it would have been easier to remove or hide them.

There are at least fifty-eight Tudor buildings left in the centre of the city and twelve of these have recently been discovered by historian Gertie Keane. Another twenty may also have Tudor origins, but this has not been confirmed due to difficulty of access and other issues. Most houses on the Parade, Rose Inn Street, High Street, Parliament Street, Irishtown, Dean Street and Coach Road have elements of Tudor in them. Many are cherished by their owners, like the wonderful Maibe Carey on Parliament Street, whose kitchen dates back to around 1550.

Jealousy was rampant at the time these buildings were being constructed. The bigger the house and gardens you had, the higher your social standing, and the most desirable place to have your Tudor house, based on continental and English architecture, was clearly between Kilkenny Castle and St Canice's Cathedral. For example, Parliament Street is totally Tudor at the back, as can be seen in the side-back wall of the building which houses The Italian Connection restaurant. Another strong example of Tudor architecture in this area is the entrance to the Butter Slip. The stonework dates from the late 1500s, but the top has been plastered over – it is about time it was re-exposed. And wouldn't it be lovely to re-associate with their Tudor homes in the city centre the six family plaques embedded in a wall at St Mary's Church? The plaques display the original families' crests, and were a way of showing off one's status in image form to the largely illiterate population of the time.

So the next time you walk in the centre of the city be aware that you are walking in Tudorland.

Clapper Bridge

I f ever there was a heritage gem that was hidden, forgotten about and left to deteriorate, then it is the Clapper Bridge close to Little Venice. Where, you ask? For over 800 years this narrow pedestrian footbridge was used by the people of Graignamanagh to cross the rich and clean River Duiske as it meandered its way into the River Barrow from Brandon Hill.

To begin to appreciate the story of the Clapper Bridge you have to look at the long association between the town and the Cistercian monks of Duiske Abbey who first constructed the bridge on the site. The Clapper Bridge crossed the river on the shortest route between the thirteenth-century abbey and its mills. Then it became the walkway for the local people and remained so for hundreds of years. While the Barrow has had a major impact on the lives of the people of Graignamanagh, the Duiske seems closer to their hearts, because they washed in it and it was at their back doors (hence the nickname Little Venice). But when it floods, the Duiske causes chaos and many houses are filled with water and silt: these days people who choose to live in the town centre and contribute to the vitality of the urban core can't get insurance for their homes or their shops.

How, you ask, could this abandonment happen? Disgraceful is a harsh word and one not to be used lightly. However, when you consider the history attached to this place and its crucial part in the development of one of the most beautiful towns in Ireland, it is apt. There have been promises made by the County Council and by others to do something about it. Civic-minded souls in Graignamanagh Historical Society such as Owen Doyle, Colm Walsh, Billy Hoare and others have done their best to highlight its plight, as have politicians such as Ann Phelan, TD, and Councillor Tommy Prendergast. But their protestations have had the same effect on the powers that be as the droppings of a swallow on the water levels of the Grand Cooley dam in Washington State. Now it appears that the central stone of the bridge has gone, but it does not seem to be in the bed of the river. Was it washed away? A piece of limestone that size would not flow downstream. If it was taken, who would do such a thing? No one seems to know.

Many people think that Graignamanagh is suffering because it is on the border of the county, away from the centre of power in Kilkenny city. It may not be true, but if ever there was a case for positive discrimination, it is here. And there is no point in asking the OPW to get involved because all they will do is put up a plaque stating that the monument is in the care of the Commissioners of Public Works. Why the Clapper Bridge is not already a national monument is beyond me. Would a world-class heritage gem like this, together with the waterfall, Lady's Well and the old walkway from Cushendale Woollen Mills to Duiske Abbey be left in this state if they were in Kilkenny city?

If this area was brought back to life it would draw people and could do what the last government's urban renewal scheme failed to do – spark a revival in the centre of the town. Why not make a trail of the Duiske from where it rises on majestic Brandon Hill, the highest point in County Kilkenny, to the mill and then the abbey, walking over the Clapper Bridge?

Fiddown Nature Reserve

County Kilkenny boasts a secret woodland, so full of native Irish trees, unusual grasses and reeds that it has been designated a sanctuary with national and international protection. An inland island, where otters thrive and kingfishers dive, and where visitors like reed warblers and swallows spend their long summer holidays, it is a kind of Shangri-La for the animal and plant kingdom.

Fiddown is a 150-acre national nature reserve like no other. The words of W. B. Yeats' poem, 'The Song of Wandering Aengus' came flowing back as I stepped onto Fiddown Island on an unusually sunny Wednesday morning in early May. The great bard wrote:

> I went out to the hazel wood;
> Because a fire was in my head;
> And cut and peeled a hazel wand
> And hooked a berry to a thread;
> And when white moths were on the wing,
> And moth-like stars were flickering out,
> I dropped the berry in a stream
> And caught a little silver trout.

Hazel is by no means the most prosperous tree in the Sicily-shaped island sanctuary on the lower reaches of the River Suir. It is more closely associated with the willow (sally), and many people still call it the Sally Island to this day. There was a huge tradition of basket making from the sally in the area, and in the summer months residents would go in large numbers to the island, possibly from as early as the pre-Christian era right up to the nineteenth century. Sometimes they would make a day of it with a working picnic, and maybe stop off for a few drinks in Meade's famous Toll Bridge Tavern on the Kilkenny side of the river. Sally rods were also used in the thatching of the cottages of Licketstown, Aglish and the area around Mooncoin and Carrigeen.

Fiddown Island is far more famous in biological and botanical terms, however, than as the provider of thatch for cottages in South Kilkenny. It was part of the blanket of forest which once covered the entire island, long before Christianity, going back to the Tuatha de Danann, stories of whom have a strong association with the island. When the glaciers receded, two branches of what was to become the Suir formed around this section of land, creating a wooded island. This type of wet woodland along a river is rare in Ireland and the example found at Fiddown is the best in the country.

There is an oral tradition that the island was used by the druids, who concocted potions and remedies from the plants still found there, like water figwort, wild angelica (which you pay a fortune for in cosmetic shops), ragwort, marsh marigold, hemlock, water dropwort, summer snowflake and the sweet-smelling wild garlic. What we can be certain of is that monks used the island. According to local historian Mary O'Shea, reclusive hermits were sent there from nearby abbeys, including Tybroughney, to pray in solitude for the rest of their brothers and for generous benefactors. There is also a shocking rumour that in the past the island was used by poachers of wild Atlantic salmon to avoid detection by the authorities.

But it is the native trees still growing here that are probably one of Fiddown's most important resources. Goat, almond and osier willows, guelder rose and hazel are the main species. It is also a haven for rarely seen Irish fauna. People living on both the Portlaw (Waterford) side and on the County Kilkenny side of the river say that on a summer's evening they can see the otters feeding on trout, salmon and other rarer fish species making their way up and down the tidal River Suir, using the dense vegetation as camouflage.

If you walk twenty yards off the busy Fiddown Bridge, the noise of the traffic fades away as you plod your course through the vegetation and into an unknown world, like something out of a South American rainforest, without the heat or the leeches. The alluvial soil here is like a dark sand and while it is great for drainage on riverbank fields, it is hard to move in.

Feathered visitors to Fiddown arrive from Africa, and

the appearance of the willow warblers and grasshopper warblers to the island marks the beginning of summer. Swallows also stop off here on their way back from North Africa before heading to the exact place where they were hatched, and return year after year. Other birds such as owls and fowl use it all year long while wintering teal, cormorants, whooper swans, water rails, long-tailed tits and breeding blackcaps are regulars. Seasonal visitors also include reed buntings, sedge warblers, mute swans, whitethroats, chiffchaffs, grey wagtails, rails, moorhens, coots, little grebes, herons and little egrets. Greylag geese are known to use land further downstream on the Waterford side of the river. Golden plovers and lapwings are found in the area in winter. And of course another protected species, Daubenton's bat, are regulars.

The River Suir is rich in nutrients and, with water quality improving every year in the last decade, it supports Atlantic salmon and Twaite shad, which migrate upstream to spawn in the Carrick-on-Suir area. These two species are internationally protected. Other 'residents' include smelt and 'slob' or estuarine trout. And of course there are the Fiddown Island snails.

Fiddown may be a hidden gem of a different kind from the rest of those in this book, but that doesn't make it any the less worthy of inclusion here.

Magdalene Castle

Magdalene Castle on Maudlin Street, off John Street, in the centre of Kilkenny (which got its name because it was written down phonetically), was the medieval predecessor to the Betty Ford Clinic in America. Members of the higher echelons of society went to recuperate from various conditions and to deal with old age and, although never mentioned, alcohol addiction. Well-heeled patients were provided with their own private living space, garden and orchard. It acted as a retirement home for rich burgesses from families such as the Rothes, Langtons and Shees. The plush rooms in Magdalene Castle were reserved for the very wealthiest of citizens and we also know from recent archaeological digs on the street that their diet was mainly beef, mutton, bacon and some wildfowl. However, there is no sign of fish – which is a little unusual when you consider that the castle is right next to the River Nore.

Magdalene Castle was named after Mary Magdalene, the woman of dubious virtue befriended by Christ who has always been associated with the care of lepers and other outcasts in society. In medieval lore in particular, sexual excess and prostitution were connected with leprosy, and many leper houses were dedicated to her. William Marshall, the Norman responsible for Kilkenny Castle in the early thirteenth century, built the original structure. It is not clear if it initially formed part of the Kilkenny's main defences, but it certainly protected the city's outer precincts and also kept the lepers and other patients away from the main population. This wonderful example of a Norman castle was used at various stages as a kind of workhouse, nursing home, castle and 'community centre' and formed the backdrop to a number of excellent nineteenth-century novels.

The castle is inextricably linked to St Stephen's Grave-yard adjacent to it, to get to which you pass by wonderful rows of immaculately kept terraced houses that link it and the castle, while in the background you have the River Nore, the weir and, straight across the river, Ormonde Mills. Nobody on the street can remember when the metal gate at the side of the structure was last opened but the graveyard has been used from time to time to store artefacts and material that has fallen from the top of the castle. It also held a number of the grave slabs taken from the River Nore as part of the city's flood-relief scheme, but no one is sure what has happened to them. It is the resting place of Kilkenny's most famous writer, John Banim, but although there is a small plaque on the outside wall on the Dublin Road side telling you his grave is located there, finding the plot itself is difficult.

To counteract that, there is a fierce pride of this place

in Maudlin Street and its environs – there is not one piece of graffiti on the castle and no one ever seems to have got inside the small, gated opening at the side of the castle. Local people will always stop and chat to visitors who stumble across this hidden gem of the city. People mistakenly think that a turret two hundred yards down towards John Street had something to do with the castle but it did not: it either formed part of a defence wall from St John's Priory or was part of the old city wall.

Historical and archaeological evidence garnered from human bones on a site next to the castle suggests that leprosy arrived in Kilkenny in the tenth or eleventh century. (The dig was carried out as part of the planning permission for a small development.) In the Middle Ages, before the advances of modern medicine, any disfiguring skin disease was thought to have been caused by leprosy. But in fact it may not have been quite as prevalent as was thought: where large amounts of medieval skeletons have been investigated only around 2–3 per cent show evidence of the disease. Lepers were usually confined to leper hospitals and were housed with those who were poor, sick and desperate enough to risk infection. The treatment involved long-term isolation, with no visitors allowed, and this often led to divorce for married sufferers. Under the law of the church lepers were considered dead and had no rights. By the sixteenth century the incidence of leprosy had declined dramatically, largely because anyone who was weak or sick had been wiped out by the 1348–49 Black Death.

The castle, then known as Our Hospital of St Mary Magdalene, was certainly in existence by 1327 and it quickly became one of the principal leper houses in medieval Ireland. Then, in the fifteenth century its function and clients changed, becoming a hospital where the upper classes had their illnesses attended to. Like most other hospitals it was somewhat remote from the town, on the edge of the suburb of St John's, and surrounded by high walls. Entrance into its precinct was strictly controlled through a gatehouse connected with the castle. Inside the defended precinct there was also a chapel, a graveyard (now St Stephen's) and the suite of hospital buildings. The hospital held fifty acres of farmland in what is now the townland of Maudlin, half a mile to the east.

Right from its foundation it must have been overrun with patients, as the first half of the fourteenth century saw Ireland suffer from famine, disease, war and finally the Black Death. Half of Kilkenny's population perished in this plague. Because the hospital was run by a monastic order, however, it was dissolved by order of Henry VIII in 1541. At that time the castle was described as follows: 'a small castle roofed with tiles, which was built for the defence of the lepers and dwellers in the suburbs, this is now empty and worth nothing'. Largely empty since that time, it is nonetheless an important part in the history of the city.

Kilkenny Castle

The final two stories in the book might come as a bit of a surprise to readers when the title *Hidden Kilkenny* is considered. Both the castle and St Canice's are very evident in Kilkenny's landscape. However, it is my hope in these two pieces to illuminate the less well-known aspects of these glorious monuments and uncover hidden gems of their history, which the casual observer may not notice.

Oliver Cromwell continues to receive a lot of bad press for his antics while in Ireland during the seventeenth century. He was responsible for a lot of destruction, particularly in Kilkenny, but the people of the city, in a strange way, owe him a debt of gratitude. His forces were responsible for knocking down the wall of the castle that protected it from the east. When James Butler, 1st Duke of Ormonde, went back after Cromwell died, he decided to leave it the way it was because it opened up the countryside. With the introduction of cannons, castle walls were no longer impregnable and were not as important as they once were, so he opted instead to go for a French chateau style when remodelling. At the height of their influence, the Butlers had over 20,000 acres and the 'park' ran to hundreds of acres. When the castle was handed over to the state in 1967 for the nominal sum of £50, however, all that was left of the parkland was fifteen acres.

The Marquis of Ormonde then bought back some of the adjoining land and gave it to the state so that today we have just over fifty-two acres of park in the centre of a medieval city. When you walk into the castle and look to your right, you see acres of parkland that, if Cromwell hadn't come, would never have been opened up. The freedom to roam around the castle grounds is part of the real attraction of the place.

The first stone castle on this site, like Magdelene Castle, was built for William Marshall. It was constructed on the site of an earlier timber structure, probably during the first decade of the thirteenth century. Although little of this remains, recent excavations revealed a massive stone batter at the base of the walls, which served as a defensive measure that descended into the dry ditch or moat, on the outer faces of the surviving curtain walls. Two postern gates were also uncovered and one of these can be seen to the right of the main gateway before you enter the castle.

In 1391 James Butler purchased the castle and this family retained its ownership of it until 1967. Over their centuries of ownership the castle went through various phases of rebuilding and remodelling, and the building that we see today is a mixture of numerous architectural styles, from the moated Norman fortress, through the seventeenth-century classical gateway, to the nineteenth-century rebuilding and remodelling which introduced the castellated baronial style. The most modern addition is the conference centre housed within the medieval fabric of the Parade Tower.

Perhaps the best way to appreciate the castle as it is today is to walk down to John's Bridge at night; under floodlights its sheer scale, size and majesty hit you. Then walk from there back up the Parade. On your left is the outer wall protecting the Rose Garden (Celtic-cross shaped) and the tasteful street lighting of the new, rejuvenated Parade is a good preparation for the entrance to the castle with its massive wooden doors. The gateway was completed in the 1700s and it has large Corinthian pilasters on either side. Above the gateway is the brightly coloured Butler–Ormonde crest that inspired fear, and commanded respect, all over the island during the height of that family's power. When the castle was used as a residence, a porter or gatekeeper would have been on duty at all times and would probably have lived in small rooms within the gateway. Some years ago this area was refurbished as part of the Parade Tower Conference Centre and to your right, under the wall, as well as the postern door, you will see the remains of the excavated dry ditch or moat that was filled in during the seventeenth century to enable the construction of this gateway in the curtain wall. Also note the heavy sloping batter of the walls and the garderobe chute.

The main area of the castle forms the route of official tours, which concentrate on the Victorian era from 1838 to 1900. However, just as interesting is the Butler Gallery in the basement (which will move in a few years' time to new premises, Evans Home, off John Street) and the old kitchen complete with bells at the end of the west wing where you can get tea, coffee and hot food. It's like a scene from *Downton Abbey* or *Upstairs Downstairs*. The huge oven is still in the kitchen and a large window in the basement facing onto the castle park floods the room with light. On the opposite side of the castle, the medieval room is fascinating with its loopholes.

But perhaps most interesting is the Long Gallery, also known as the Picture Gallery. It is now home to many marvellous things, although most attention centres on the rather plain-looking portraits of the Butlers of Ormonde that adorn the walls, including a close relation of the ill-fated Princess Diana. But above their heads is the best artistic invention in the history of Kilkenny. It is fascinating how an Englishman, John Hungerford Pollen, an Anglican clergyman who converted to Catholicism, was able to tap into the Irish psyche and come up with almost Celtic motifs for the structure of this room. As you enter the Picture Gallery and look up, you see dark pastures with heavy clumps of grass and other vegetation in which all sorts of strange creatures lurk, and slowly the twisty trees rise above the ground, adder-like; their branches, without leaves, rise up to a grey December sky.

Just above is the gallery's long central glazed corridor and as you walk along you see many different shades of turquoise and russet red. Regrettably time has not been kind to the wooden panelling – much of the detail is hard to distinguish twenty feet below on the newly lacquered and polished wooden parquet floor of this amazing space. It was built as a public gallery for the people of Kilkenny in the nineteenth century, but the idea never really caught on because access was limited and people had no real appreciation of the place.

Every few yards there are little holes cut in the wood, mainly shaped like shamrocks or clover, and at one time, coloured glass was placed in the holes so that, when light passed through the openings, it gave the garden scene a life of its own. What a pity this is not recreated now. The 'roof garden' culminates in a wonderful flowing cataract (the idea stolen from Tennyson) with doves, white rabbits and other creatures, mythical and real, and, as with many of the works from this period, the imagery is all to do with the hunt. It has been said disparagingly that some of the hunt creatures, hogs and such like, are likenesses of those in the framed paintings on the wall below.

My poor description of the work by John Hungerford Pollen does not do justice to it. Despite the fact that his work was described by a contemporary in the once important journal of that period, *The Irish Builder*, as 'a roof probably intended to be Byzantine but merely bizarre', this amazing creation is intoxicating, spiritually uplifting and highly unusual. The ceiling of the Long Gallery at Kilkenny Castle is worth a second and third look. The workmanship of the man is wonderful. Countrywomen adorn the arched beams that hold up the roof and near the ninth beam there is a painting of a young boy, believed to be John Pollen's son. If you really want to enjoy the Picture Gallery experience, just put on your headphones and play something by Ennio Morricone from *The Mission* or, if you are a traditionalist, something from Stockton's Wing. Pollen also designed the white Carrara marble fireplace in the centre of the gallery. It is a joy to stroll around and the people of Kilkenny are blessed to have such a space.

In a way we are lucky that this roof even exists, as it was bad planning and workmanship that led to the development of this space. When the gallery was originally built, it was given a flat roof. However, the roof began to leak and the distinguished architectural firm of Deane and Woodward was called in during the 1860s to make changes to the overall design. These changes included the insertion of four bay windows in the west wall and the blocking up of the eight existing windows, while another window was added to the east wall. Where did the money come from for such a grandiose scheme? It's a little complicated, but we are indebted to the OPW for supplying the answer, put together so succinctly:

It was during the nineteenth century that the Ormonde's reached the apogee of power, position, and estates. The long drawn out dispute over the Ormonde inheritance had ended with an arranged marriage between Elizabeth Preston (1615–84), granddaughter of Thomas, the 10th Earl, and her cousin James Butler (1610–88), 12th Earl of Ormonde, later 1st Marquess and 1st Duke of Ormonde. Ormonde, as a loyal supporter of the beleaguered King Charles I, had been made commander-in-chief of the king's forces in Ireland in 1641. Following the royalists' defeat at the hands of the Cromwellian army, Ormonde crossed to France and spent another decade travelling about Northern Europe with the exiled king, Charles II. After the restoration of Charles II to the throne of England, Ormonde was elevated to a dukedom for his loyal service to the Stuart monarchy. As Ireland's sole duke and viceroy, Ormonde had reached the pinnacle of aristocratic society in the country.

When another James Butler (1665–1745) succeeded his grandfather as second duke of Ormonde, he came into a vast inheritance from both of his grandparents. Their son John Butler (1808–54), 2nd Marquess of Ormonde, was also deeply interested in collecting art, and during his ownership the picture gallery was built and many new paintings were acquired.

It would be a mistake to consider the castle in isolation, and to really understand castle life you have to take in all the history that surrounds it. Directly across the road is the Kilkenny Design and the Craft Council of Ireland exhibition space where gold and silversmiths still create wonderful pieces of jewellery. These are housed in what were the stables and coach house of the castle and their size reflects the grandeur of life in Kilkenny Castle. Walk through a small arched entrance in this building and you enter the maze-like gardens of Butler House, which faces on to Patrick Street. Completely refurbished by the Kilkenny Design state-run body in 1972, Butler House boasts sweeping staircases, magnificent plastered ceilings and marble fireplaces. Known as the dower house of Kilkenny Castle, it was home to Lady Eleanor Butler after the death of her husband Walter in 1783. Lady Eleanor was the mother of John, the 17th Earl of Ormonde. Her daughter, also Eleanor, and Sarah Ponsonby became known as the 'Ladies of Llangollen' when they fled from their families in 1778 rather than face the possibility of unwanted marriages and ended up settling near the town of Llangollen in Wales. In the nineteenth century this house was used as a residence by the Earl when the castle was under reconstruction and in 1870 was the scene of the meetings of the Royal Historical and Archaeological Association of Ireland. Today it is one of Kilkenny's best surviving examples of Georgian architecture.

St Canice's Cathedral

What began as a rather modest monastic settlement, founded by Saint Canice in the sixth century, quickly became an ecclesiastical and political capital, a place where the Gaelic kings of Ossory had a palace up to the ninth century. When these kings and their druids were driven off, a cathedral was eventually constructed on the clay where royalty, lords, bishops, abbots and commoners had been interred. Just six steps away the city's oldest building, the 100-foot tall round tower, has dominated the site for over 900 years and was donated to the clergy in 849 by O'Carroll, King of Leinster.

Although the cathedral measures just 212 feet in length, it is full of priceless historical, archaeological and social data. There are tombs of various Butlers – lords, dukes and marquises of Ormonde – and of course it is the resting place of Piers and Margaret Butler, who really put the Butler name on the map, as we saw earlier in the story of Grannagh Castle. Here, too, lie the remains of a direct ancestor of US President Barack Obama, Bishop John Kearney.

Dame Alice Kyteler haunts the place – literally – and it was here that her son, William Outlaw, kept his promise to a cranky Bishop Ledred in the fourteenth century to repair the cathedral roof. This was to make up for his mother's alleged crimes and the fact that she escaped before they could burn her at the stake. He loaded the roof deliberately with lead to ensure it would fall, as it did, bringing with it the central tower and causing devastation below.

The cathedral continues to be a place of worship and people come from all over the world to pray for their ancestors buried within the precincts. When I walk through the arch and through the beautifully ornate wooden doors of the cathedral, I am reminded of T. S. Eliot's *Murder in the Cathedral* and the assassination of Archbishop Thomas Becket in Canterbury Cathedral in 1170. Despite being a sacred place, St Canice's has been the subject of intrigue, rows and feuds (which simmer to this day) concerning who should own it – the Catholics, or the current incumbents, the Church of Ireland. The latter does a superb job of conserving this splendid cathedral and it has ensured that surviving fragments of a Romanesque church that accompanied the round tower as part of an ornate structure built in the twelfth century are preserved. Following the Anglo-Norman conquest this church was torn down and replaced by the great cathedral that stands to this day.

Its status as the diocesan see coupled with rich patronage from the city's nobility led to the construction of one of Ireland's largest and finest medieval cathedrals. However, what makes St Canice's truly unique in Ireland is that its original close survives intact, complete with its boundaries, gatehouse, bishop's palace and a suite of buildings that housed the cathedral dignitaries. By European standards, St Canice's is modest in both size and elaboration; nevertheless, it is its very scale and simplicity that makes it such an attractive prospect. Since its completion in 1285 there have been no significant additions or surviving alterations.

St Canice's is also a very special site for archaeology. It was here that James Graves, one of the first great Irish archaeologists, worked, researched and was buried in the nineteenth century. The site also enshrines a vast trove of information on the unwritten past, the raw material of archaeology.

Excavations have unearthed skeletons of some of the first monks who dwelt on the site as well as evidence for what they ate: berries, beef and biscuits were mainstays! Toilet facilities included a fancy stone-lined loo, and food was stored in elaborate stone-lined underground passages called souterrains. The making of combs and wood-turning were important monastic industries and the organisation of the ecclesiastical settlement appears to be the Kilkenny version of the holy city of Jerusalem!

A geophysical survey has identified what may have been the royal palace of the Gaelic kings of Ossory near the round tower and the diocesan palace that was built by Bishop Ledred at the time of the Black Death and has been hidden behind Georgian and Victorian modifications. Cells in which medieval hermits were encased have been found on the site; in the Middle Ages, such 'anchorite cells' were a common feature and no self-respecting cathedral was without them.

Thousands of artefacts from all eras have been recovered from the site: stained glass from the famous east window that Cromwell smashed; exotic ceramics from France, England and Spain; floor tiles decorated with lashing beasts; medieval dowled and morticed roof-timbers; and pieces of finely made early medieval combs, to name but a few. St Canice's is Kilkenny's Sacré Coeur.

In essence, St Canice's Cathedral tells the story of how, for centuries, all those associated with it have worked painstakingly to maintain its beauty, and they have done a superb job, including the preservation of the round tower a few yards from it. The tower is one of only two remaining on this island where you can climb the 121 steps.

Inside the cathedral there are gems to be discovered in every corner, such as St Kieran's Chair which dates from the fourth century and was brought from Aghaboe, County Laois. The bells are magnificent; in 1674 a new set was cast and installed, while the present treble and No. 2 bells were added to the ring in 1892. They are rung every Sunday and for weddings and funerals. On New Year's Eve, the bells are muffled to ring out the old year and then the muffles are removed to ring in the new, so that the year begins with a clear peal. It's hard to beat tradition.

It's what is not in the books, guides, records or other

historical journals that is so important at St Canice's. Ghosts continue to occupy the cathedral and the close which surrounds it. There isn't just one but a number of spectres who pop up with regularity in all sorts of places. This is all taken for granted, as if it is expected by those who visit the early Gothic structure on a regular basis. Dame Alice Kyteler, who was tried for witchcraft here in the fourteenth century, often appears on the stairs under the western window of the cathedral, and she has been spotted in other places too. Around 100,000 people have been buried in the precincts of the cathedral since before Christian times and there are ghosts also in the organist's cottage and 'goings on' there that cannot be explained. Yet all these 'antics' are regarded as rather mundane by those who have encountered these phenomena of another world. For example, a person might wander into the cathedral for tea and say nonchalantly: 'I saw her again the other evening on the stairs under the west window during choir practice.'

The deanery building, to the immediate left just before you enter the cathedral grounds from the Coach Road, also has an unexplained presence. Many years ago, a resident there told me that the old bells used by the dean and his family to ring for the servants went off on a regular basis in the dead of night when no one else was around.

And as always, the shadow of the man responsible for building Kilkenny Castle, William Marshall, looms large. We should remember that when St Canice's Cathedral was built, it was a symbol of power and the Normans were foxy: they always put a castle at one end of a town or city they captured and a large church at the other to terrorise a backward, uneducated people. Contemporary records of the cathedral's construction are non-existent but it appears that it was done in two stages. Although Marshall started construction of the abbey, the earliest record from the sixteenth century awards the honour of 'first founder' to Bishop Hugh de Mapilton (1251–60) who probably built the choir, transepts and crossing tower, while the completion of the nave was left to Bishop Geoffrey de St Leger (1260–86). The lady chapel may have been rebuilt around the time the nave was finished. The completion date is often cited as 1285.

During the English Civil War (1641–51), Ireland was left in a political vacuum. In the chaos of the times, all the cathedral records were 'liberated' and, after a gap of several decades, St Canice's once again had a Roman Catholic bishop. The 'Confederation of Kilkenny' offered some stability to Ireland and prosperity to Kilkenny from 1642 to 1648. However, when Oliver Cromwell took charge of the parliamentary military campaign against Ireland, he captured Kilkenny and wrought extensive destruction on the cathedral in 1650. It remained abandoned and roofless for twelve years. The first real restoration began in 1756 under Bishop Pococke and then, between 1843 and 1877, the main restoration was carried out under the guidance of Dean Vignoles; the cathedral has remained Anglican since then.

I cannot overemphasise the significance of the close in terms of the site's overall historical value, and yet it is sometimes overlooked due to the overwhelming presence of the cathedral itself. Few people are aware of the rich social history attached to these important peripheral buildings. Many archaeological sites in Ireland are no longer 'fit for purpose' and yet remain a fascinating insight into the past. St Canice's close differs from this model insofar as it offers wonderful insights into the past but also continues to be 'fit for purpose'.

A well-kept and picturesque graveyard greatly enhances the aesthetic quality of the site and its surrounding buildings. When Dean Vignoles arrived in 1843, he found the churchyard like a wilderness and the earth so built up by a thousand years of burials that, in places, it reached almost to the windows of the cathedral. It was tidied up and the surplus earth banked against the wall at the back. A number of the cut-stone grave markers predate 1700 and the craftsmanship is of high quality. These gravestones are of great significance to the region's heritage, being solid examples of Kilkenny's architectural, artistic, archaeological and social history. Most of Ireland's churchyards have now been cleared of their untidy tombstones, but here they still add their comment and chaos to the austere formal lines of the church. Local people can enjoy the blessed peace and serenity around the graveyard while still being in the busy city.

The organist's period cottage, built in the seventeenth

century, can be found beside the library. It is a three-bay single-storey house with a half-dormer attic. It was originally built for the prebendary of Killamery and Bishop Williams converted it into an alms house in the 1660s. The organist of the cathedral and his family reside in the house to the present day but, as pointed out earlier on, they are not alone!

The library played a vital theological role in the sixteenth century. It is a two-storey building with six bays and incorporates the fabric of the original grammar school and Blackrath Castle. It carries a long tradition of ecclesiastical activities from being a manse, a grammar school, an alms house and a library. The second floor still houses the library and diocesan office and the ground floor is the home of the bishop's vicar. While many books have been sent to the Representative Church Body house in Dublin, the library still houses many important theological tomes.

Both the sanctuary and parish chapel, located off the north transept, are remarkable and an unexpected treat. Floors representing the four provinces are made from different types of marble (often taken as polished limestone). Connaught is represented by the green marble of Connemara, Leinster by the black marble of Kilkenny, Munster by the grey marble of Cork and Ulster by the red marble of Tyrone.

The sexton's house and the colonnade are semi-detached buildings and the glebe end of the sexton's house has effigies dating from the sixth century.

In the introduction to a brochure for the cathedral, the former dean of St Canice's, the much-loved Norman Lynas, says: 'Please linger in this place and drink of its serenity. It is our prayer that, as your eyes take in the visual message of this age-old church, your heart may feel the message of Christ, who is the same yesterday, today and forever.' So reverence and respect are essential when you set foot in St Canice's Cathedral.

Also available from Mercier Press

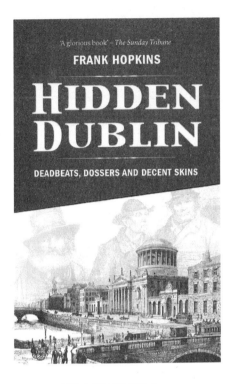

'A glorious book' – *The Sunday Tribune*

FRANK HOPKINS

HIDDEN DUBLIN

DEADBEATS, DOSSERS AND DECENT SKINS

978 1 85635 591 9

Criminal incidents, accidents, whippings, beatings, jail escapes and hangings were all part of Dublin's 'brilliant parade' in the eighteenth and nineteenth centuries, including actors, clergymen, scientists, politicians and rogues and rascals of every hue.

Hopkins describes the poverty, soup kitchens, food riots, street beggars and workhouses that were all a feature of Dublin life. He also introduces us to the weird, wonderful and often strange customs and pastimes of Dubliners stretching back to the Middle Ages, such as the 'bearing of balls' annual parade by the city's bachelors and the ritual humiliation of would-be bridegrooms at the bullring.

www.mercierpress.ie

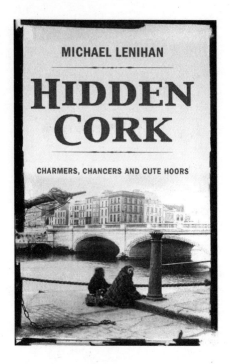

978 1 85635 686 2

In this collection, Michael Lenihan delves into the rich tapestry of Cork's history to reveal some of its most bizarre events and strangest characters. From quack doctor Baron Spolasco to the outlaw Airt Ó Laoghaire, Cork has seen some eccentric, wonderful and even some downright nasty people.

With revelations of mass graves in Bishop Lucey Park, how Jonathan Swift was awarded the freedom of the city, stories of the Gas Works' strike and the trams of the city, *Hidden Cork* opens the door on history, dumps the boring bits and brings to life the flow of time through the streets of Cork.

www.mercierpress.ie

Also available from Mercier Press

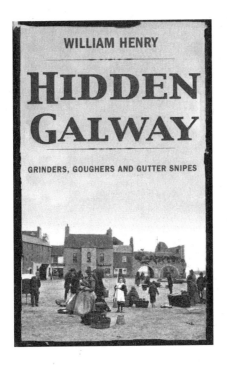

WILLIAM HENRY

HIDDEN GALWAY

GRINDERS, GOUGHERS AND GUTTER SNIPES

978 1 85635 754 8

Hidden Galway introduces the reader to a totally new history of Galway, exploring the quirky stories and fascinating rogues that history has overlooked. There are stories of disasters, such as the KLM flight which brought Galway to a standstill for over a week in 1958 and the Christmas morning tragedy of 1842, and others of extraordinary people like William from Galway, who sailed with Christopher Columbus in 1492 on his voyage of discovery. Graphic accounts of execution and murder from the City of the Tribes are told, such as the infamous Bodkin Murders, where eleven people were brutally slain in a house of horrors in one night. Included are famous and infamous bandits, highwaymen, scientists, smugglers and love stories that introduce us to the weird and wonderful customs and pastimes of the people of Galway.

www.mercierpress.ie

MERCIER PRESS

IRISH PUBLISHER · IRISH STORY

We hope you enjoyed this book.

Since 1944, Mercier Press has published books that have been critically important to Irish life and culture.

Our website is the best place to find out more information about Mercier, our books, authors, news and the best deals on a wide variety of books. Mercier tracks the best prices for our books online and we seek to offer the best value to our customers, offering free delivery within Ireland.

A large selection of Mercier's new releases and backlist are also available as ebooks. We have an ebook for everyone, with titles available for the Amazon Kindle, Sony Reader, Kobo Reader, Apple products and many more. Visit our website to find and buy our ebooks.

Sign up on our website or complete and return the form below to receive updates and special offers.

www.mercierpress.ie
www.facebook.com/mercier.press
www.twitter.com/irishpublisher

Name: _____

Email: _____

Address: _____

Mobile No.: _____

Mercier Press, Unit 3b, Oak House, Bessboro Rd, Blackrock, Cork, Ireland